D0065304

LARRY

LARRY

LARRY

THOUGHTS OF YOUTH

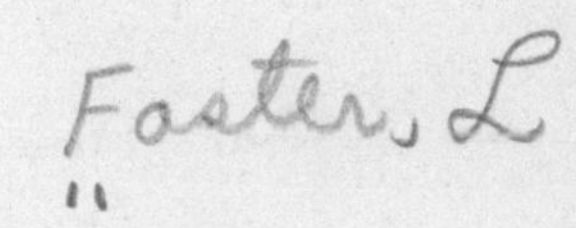

NEW YORK

THE JOHN DAY COMPANY

First Printing December 1930
Second Printing January 1931
Third Printing March 1931
Fourth Printing June 1931
Fifth Printing September 1931
Sixth Printing December 1931
Seventh Printing March 1932
Eighth Printing April 1934
Ninth Printing September 1934
Tenth Printing July 1935
Eleventh Printing May 1936

MANUFACTURED IN THE UNITED STATES OF AMERICA
FOR THE JOHN DAY CO., INC., NEW YORK
BY THE VAIL-BALLOU PRESS, INC., BINGHAMTON, N. Y.

FOREWORD

Larry was the only son of Mr. and Mrs. Thomas J. Foster of Ridgewood, N. J. He was active in school life, the Hi-Y Club, the Boy Scouts and the Methodist Episcopal Church School.

He was graduated from the Ridgewood High School when he was eighteen and entered Lafayette College in September, 1923. At the close of his sophomore year he went to Arizona for his summer's vacation.

A few days before he was to return home he was asked to pose for the picture shown opposite page 145 just as he started to ride out to watch a beautiful sunset. When he did not return a search was made. Apparently he had been sitting on the ground holding the lariat that was fastened to the saddle. Something frightened the horse and he ran, catching the lariat on Larry's wrist. He gained his feet for about fifty yards and then fell, hitting his head against a stump, causing instant death.

Usually young people are reticent about their ideals and problems, but this book opens up the mind of a young man who expressed himself clearly and frankly to himself, his family and to his friends.

A few of Larry's letters, some pages from his diary, and his philosophy have been previously printed and have created the demand for this book. This material was written with no thought of publication, and is presented without changes or explanations.

LARRY FOSTER FOUNDATION, INC.

CONTENTS

CONTENTS

ILLUSTRATIONS

LARRY

LET ME LIVE OUT MY YEARS

(*Found among Larry's poems.*)

Let me live out my years in heat of blood!
  Let me die drunken with the dreamer's wine!
Let me not see this soul-house built of mud
  Go toppling to the dust—a vacant shrine!

Let me go quickly like a candle-light
  Snuffed out just at the heydey of its glow!
Give me high noon—and let it then be night!
  Thus would I go.

And grant me when I face the grisly Thing,
  One haughty cry to pierce the gray Perhaps!
Let me be as a tune-swept fiddle-string
  That feels the Master Melody—and snaps!

JOHN G. NEIHARDT.

LAFAYETTE COLLEGE

FRESHMAN YEAR

Monday:

Bid fond and 'fectionate farewell to folks. I was invited to the Chi Phi House for tomorrow noon and to Zeta Psi tonight. They all sound Greek to me! I liked the Zetes a lot: I seemed to fit in. There is going to be one maxim which I shall adopt: "Keep your mouth shut; don't let them know how dumb you are. Listen instead."

Tuesday:

Fussed around and saw the college, which I like immensely. I wonder if out of all this crowd I shall find one real friend? Lunch at Chi Phi was nice; the fellows are fine there also. I suppose everyone is on his good behavior though. Zetes' for supper again and after a rotten vaude at Bethlehem we came back. Johnny Detjens and Bob Allen are great. Gave snap judgment and pledged Zete shortly after midnight! Instinct, maybe; I'm glad I did.

Wednesday:

Opening address in afternoon. Pajama parade at night was heaps of fun. Between soreness on my posterior region and aches from laughing I'm tired but happy. Gosh, the sophs do love to be officious! They were frosh last year, too.

Thursday:

College began. I'm going to like classes. Made a heck of a good start by flunking English!

FROM SECOND TO HIGH

Theme for Freshman English

THE relation of the steps in education to Life might be compared to the relation of the various speeds of an automobile to its efficiency, for in education Grammar School is certainly "low," High School is "intermediate," and College is "high"; each of the first two speeds being necessary to the next greater one. A man may run his automobile in first or second gear for a long time and eventually reach his destination, but think of the wasted power! His driving wheel is too small; he has a deficient education. On the other hand, a man facing a hard problem or a steep grade *must get down to fundamentals* or shift to a lower speed.

Even if one wanted to do so, it would be impossible to retain the viewpoints formed in a preparatory school. There the conceptions of athletics, scholarship, social life, and even morals are so entirely different from those of college that one is temporarily at sea on most matters. The "driving wheel" is enlarging and the process is often painful.

My "shift" from high school to Lafayette will be a transition, I hope, that will make for greater efficiency, concentration of purpose, broader vision, and a responsibility not to myself, but to Society.

To Girl [1]

Already I am sick of the color green. It is a dreadful excuse for it. Green tie, green card about six inches square dangling from your lapel, and a little black cap with a bright green button, not to mention cuffless and creaseless trousers, stamp one as a "poor damn Frosh" all over the place. The kids downtown follow us around hollering more or less uncomplimentary things, and the townspcople give us the merry ha-ha! Gee, but it really is fun for all that, because everyone pities the underdog, and we sure are that! Of course we can't wear knickers or white trousers, and only black socks.

CONFLICT

Theme for Freshman English

IT would be difficult to describe the feeling with which I first surveyed the "Hilltop" where my home for the next few years was to be made. Pleasure, expectation, and—yes, I am sure of it now—a little fear, were some of my rather mixed emotions. During the next few days I wondered vaguely when my first vivid impressions of college were to come. The old, vine-covered buildings, the sound of the

[1] Larry's salutation to a former classmate in High School.

bell on Old South, the wonderfully romantic traditions—was any one of these Lafayette? And then one day came the answer.

A sweating, grunting, cussing, heaving mass of men twisted and writhed on the ground. Those on the bottom struggled to get their hands on a short pole, and more often succeeded in getting somebody's foot in their faces. The more fortunate individuals on the outside, heedless of the fact that their weight was slowly but surely crushing those underneath, kept piling higher and faster, until the mass looked like a small volcano "in reverse," its lava streaming up instead of down its sides.

This was Lafayette! A struggle from beginning to end, yet mixed with greatest pleasure. Lafayette is but a tiny world, and is not life in this world a struggle? For the fight between right and wrong, between self-control and impulse, between duty and pleasure, Lafayette is the battleground and a glorious one!

To Girl

I hardly can wait for the time when I can walk around this dear old campus with you. Oh, you'll love it the way I do. So green, so beautifully planted with every kind of tree, so stunning in sunlight, so silvery white in the moonlight, with the mist creeping up from the city and the little lights twinkling from the dorms, and a bunch of men singing somewhere—oh, it's College Life! Not the wild parties that so many think represent the "life" of a college, but the spirit of men, the old traditions that make you remember that fifty and sixty years ago students were walking the same paths,

This dear old Campus, so beautifully planted with every kind of tree. Oh, you'll love it the way I do.

singing the same songs, and loving the same old "college on the Hill."

I haven't mentioned the game with Pitt. We were stunned, that's all. We sat around the house like mummies, dumb and almost tearful. We wanted that game so badly! Banny, the right end, didn't come home with the team because he is the one who fumbled twice with the ball over Pitt's line! Can you imagine the rotten luck? Ernst, the quarter, threw two almost perfect passes to him, and once in front and once over the line, he dropped the ball, and so made the pass incomplete. I wouldn't be that man for a million dollars. He was in line for the All-American team and of course now is out of it. But even Pitt acknowledged that we outplayed them, beginning in the second quarter. A moral victory, however, does not go down in history as a rule!

"IF YOU CAN MEET WITH TRIUMPH AND DISASTER . . ."

Theme for Freshman English

FOR nearly three quarters Lafayette had pushed her adversary back, ever toward her goal, and now the Maroon team was facing a possible score. The eleven men who strained into position were going to put that ball over the line or go down fighting. The sudden hush in the stands made audible the voice of the quarterback. Sharp, penetrating, driving, pleading, it sounded a clarion call of defiance to the grim line of black-jerseyed men who tensely awaited the play. "Twenty-nine, thirty-seven, eighteen—"

A typical New York mist hung like a pall over the Polo Grounds; a huge gray curtain that closed in the stands oppressively. The turf-torn field was beginning to grow hazy and the outlines dim and uncertain. There! Ernst had the ball! He was running back—he would pass—*get that ball*—oh!

The crowd was on its feet cheering madly, jumping up and down hysterically, shrieking, yelling, delirious with joy, for "Chick" had caught the ball and was calmly sitting on it over the goal line! Wait—the sudden hush—what? Back twenty yards—out of bounds! The voice in the stand changed to one of menace; a low muttering that was swelling into a dull roar, threatening violence and disaster—

Oh, Lafayette, now you can prove that good sportsmanship is a component of your cosmos, a vital fundamental of your spirit. Now you can prove that "you can meet with Triumph and Disaster, and treat those two impostors just the same!"

To Girl

Today was the first time that I was in scrimmage and believe me *it is fun!* O man! to feel all that power and snap banging into you, and to know that you have to forget yourself and hit 'em hard! That's the joy of it. Up till now I stuck to football because I was ashamed to quit, not because I liked the drill and signal practice. But now, once I've felt the thrill of the thing, I will stick till death do us part! It is going to be hard, too, for "Freshman Players" starts this Friday in the afternoon.

Work is going splendidly and Bob and I are getting closer together every day. He is out for the "Lafayette" and artist on the "Lyre" board. Both of us are out for the Glee Club, and that starts soon. Today Herb Brown, Zete and captain of debating, asked me to try out for the latter. I'm sure undecided for I mustn't get in too many activities.

Congratulations about your joining the Mandolin Club. While I talk about these things you do them! "Head of the class!"

Two nice things have happened. I made Frosh Players by giving some lines from "Maker of Dreams" (Pierrot's part), and I made the Glee Club (until the next cut).

We are getting along famously—or rather notoriously. I'll stay in College. I have to plug like the dickens to get the stuff, but the plugging is like a game. The professor moves—then I move—and always I'm "it." But I'll checkmate him yet.

UNDERSTANDING

Theme for Freshman English

A SPEAKER once said that in spite of the fact that the "little red schoolhouse" floggings of bygone days are now obsolete and frowned upon, many a man is more "polished" now because of a "hardwood finish" in his youth. Today, however, other forces than birch rods contribute to a professor's unpopularity. Is he arrogant or domineering in the classroom? Does he expect too much from students? Does he treat the men like children? Above all, does he misinterpret, misconstrue actions and words; does he lack understanding? If he does he is sure to be as unpopular as a well-developed case of measles.

One of the most amazing relations between the student and his professor is the attitude that they have for each other outside of class. To the man coming from high school where the teacher is his natural enemy in *or* out of school, the sight of a professor and a student hobnobbing at a bridge game until early in the morning, and then the same professor publicly calling down the same student the next day for being unprepared, is nothing short of bewildering.

The college professor who treats the students like men, who understands, is sure to be the one who is truly popular.

To Girl

Do you mind if I talk to you a little while tonight? The fact is that I spent thirty cents and three hours and have brought very little in return. You see, for the last seventeen years I have had pretty smooth sailing and only lately have I realized that college is not quite up to the ideals we all hear about. Boy, am I disconnected and raving? Mais oui!

Tonight we had Glee rehearsal and had a heck of a lot of fun. We have been learning all the old songs before starting on any new ones. Then G——, dandy fellow, and F—— and I went downtown, the first time for me in two weeks. I was to meet another fellow, and missed him completely. I got soaked, for it sure was raining, and so I went with G—— and F—— to a bar where the latter likes to indulge. You know Easton is about the "wettest" place in Pennsylvania and one can get anything one wants at all times. I was interested but went out again to look for Smithy. When I returned they had left the bar and after half an hour I located them in the vaude.

It wasn't so very bad, but I wasn't so crazy about it by any means, and I sat next to F—— who had a breath that would knock most people over. Not that *I* can stand it so well! The whole affair was so far from what I consider a good time that it sort of sickened me. And afterwards two fellows from another house offered us some lovely smelling whisky just to sort of cap the climax. Wet, disgusted, lonesome for old friends and especially you, I *had* to write before I went to sleep. So now, it being 11:45 P. X., I am writing on a drawing board in my own room because Norm is sleeping in the study and doesn't want the light on. I'm just as comfortable as if I had the measles.

You see here is the problem; how can I keep my respect for a man who ruins his body, brain and soul for and with a little fool "fire-water" no matter how much I like him when he's sober? I wouldn't care if he hurt only himself, but think of the people and places he *is* hurting! Folks, fraternity brothers, friends, college and society in general, because *he is breaking a law*. I may be very old-fashioned, but when a law is in the constitution I believe it is an act of treason to break it! Now, by golly, either I'm wrong or I'm right, and there is no compromise.

There, I've poured out all my troubles tonight, and I sure feel better. You'll understand, you always do, that it is just something which troubles me a bit, and after a while I'll laugh at myself for worrying about it. But I'm glad that I have you to tell. "If I can keep my head when all about me—"

Now can you keep a secret? You had better for I shall not tell you otherwise. You are alone in this dark secret. I have not told mother or father, but you, you will understand that I am not increasing my hat size, etc.

I had the highest mark in Public Speaking of the eighty-some fellows in the section. It was B and I missed an A by one lone recitation that I should have had easily. There, I've been busting to proclaim it from the housetops, and now I feel better. And that is not all. My average is the highest of the "pledges" in the House, and the Prof himself congratulated me! Now tell me that I am an egotistic fool and I'll agree with you.

Oh, but I'm proud of you! If I should sign my name and send this letter I would have said everything that I might possibly say to you. For I am proud I know you, proud that you are my finest friend, and proud that you like me enough to write me.

You know, about the only time in my life when I was nearly homesick was when I was coming back on the train. I wasn't so well over the week-end (of course it had to be the first time this year when I was home) and I was feeling very badly coming back here, and I couldn't help thinking about you and the fun I had the night before. I wanted to turn the train around and go back to you pronto.

Now we'll come back to Mlle. la Presidente! Frankly, I'm tickled stiff and if you wouldn't think that I was "throwing an awful line" I could say it much better than that, for "tickled stiff" is a very meager expression for a description of my feelings. Let me tell you the happy details of my sudden knowledge.

I was asleep at a few minutes after eleven (per instructions) and at 11:35 somebody started mauling me and told me I was wanted on the 'phone. I'm afraid I wasn't exactly polite to my awakener but I stumbled to the 'phone. Then I came to with a shock for the man said, "Telegram from New London." Heavens! Girl hurt? Soccer? You know the things one always thinks of. Then: "Girl elected president of class, signed—the other Ridgewoodites." I could have hugged the whole delegation! Then I let out a yell, and was promptly told to leave this world by several sleepy voices.

When they made you the "head of the class" they put new pep into me. I feel as if I could lick the world, and to prove it I'll get an A in math.

I told you that Hart had made dates with three girls for us (Hart, Bob, Tinsman and I) for last night, so that we could meet them before the dance. Well, we went for them and then we all went to the home of one of the girls, Ada Somebody (I can't spell it) where we danced for a while. All three girls are juniors in the High School and are very nice; in fact they are nicer than the average by a good deal. Perhaps it is because they are so unsophisticated! Anyway we played bridge with Mr. and Mrs. Whitzell (something like that) who are very fine people. Mrs. Whitzell is especially nice, and she kept the bunch pepped up every minute. After we had some sandwiches and cocoa she went to the piano and played our Alma Mater and other songs and we all sang. It really was lots of fun. It was so nice and different from most parties, where the mother and father never show themselves for fear they are butting in. I am afraid that I am hopelessly simple and out of fashion, and uncollegian, but I can't enjoy a gang that lives on nothing but mushing and necking and who have absolutely nothing inside their upper stories but nonsense.

The Whitzells told me that I was welcome at their home at any time so I have a nice place to go when I need to talk.

Saturday was the most exciting day in my young and eventful life. The campus was just seething with suspense and was covered with posters looking something like this

BE AT
LEHIGH

They may be read both ways: "Be at Lehigh" and "Beat Lehigh."

Friday night was the big smoker that is always held before the Lehigh game. Really I have never known what enthusiasm was until I attended that meeting. Anyway, we decided to beat Lehigh, and so yesterday we carried out our word.

The excitement and suspense was awful and several of the faculty excused the last classes because the men were almost wild. We saw the game next, and it *was* a game! Lehigh fought like fury and beat us in the first half. That made us mad, so we came back in the second and ran up thirteen points in the last quarter. We almost went wild.

FIRES

Theme for English

For some time last summer I was camping in the mountains with an old woodsman, a man full of fascinating stories of adventure and travel. One night while we were sitting around our little "friendship fire" he said rather pensively:

"There is a belief among many solitary woodsmen that every color or tint to which a tree is exposed during its life glows in the fire when that tree is burned." He stopped to relight his pipe with a burning twig. "Look deep into the coals and you can find the pinks and violets of dawn, the blueness of the sky, the burning brightness of the noonday sun, the angry black of a thundercloud, the crimson of the sunset, the silver radiance of the moonlight, the brilliant transparency of the stars . . ."

I returned in time to see the Lafayette victory bonfire. Strangely, it recalled to me that little fire in the mountains; one a foot high, the other a hundred. Looking into those leaping flames I saw embodied there the marvelous colors of the love and passion of Lafayette's alumni; the deep blues of the loyalty of her students; and, above all, the brilliant whiteness of her purity and spirit!

To Girl

You know, I doubt if you have ever experienced the feeling that you are an "also-ran." I hope you never do. It used to hurt my feelings dreadfully, and I was blue as blue could be when I saw fellows going up the aisle in Chapel to get their letters. Now I guess that I am a bit hardened to it, and whenever I go out it is with the cold and unromantic knowledge that I will have to give my best and stick like glue—and then get bounced. Please don't think that I have become discouraged; I realize that some day I will make *some* team—for all I know checkers or chess.

When I do get a bit disgusted sometimes I read that little poem "Thinking"—it ends like this:

"Life's battles don't always go
To the stronger or faster man;
But soon or late the man who wins,
Is the man who thinks he can!" [1]

[1] "Thinking," by Walter Wintle.

FRESHMAN YEAR

RESULTS

Theme for English

A PREACHER's wife once wanted to surprise her husband on his birthday. In the evening she called in several of the "pillars" of the church and, after ushering them into a dark room, called her husband to come and strike a light. He agreed rather ungraciously, and while striking the match burned his finger—and swore.

That minister had sworn before!

To the majority of people only the *results* of training are seen, and football is a game played in four quarters of fifteen minutes each. On the field, the whistle before the first kick and after the allotted time has elapsed, is the alpha and omega of that greatest of fall sports. To one who knows the training is a long, hard and often uninteresting drudgery, brisk scrimmages and games being the only relief from the monotony of exercises and signal practice. Training is not only for aggressiveness, but for defense. Trained muscles are necessary to withstand bruises and knockouts, for they have the coördination with the nervous system that the untrained muscles have not.

Preparedness is a fundamental principle of football, and leaving the field of sports, of success in any branch of work. The analogy may be extended to the "knockout," for the man with training and experience can take a failure with a smile and come back—to win.

LARRY

To Girl

I am out for gym again since the basketball cut left me in the cold, cold world, and really I enjoy it more and more. The idea of building up a body in all respects appeals to me a lot. Tonight I am going to talk with Doc Bruce, the physical trainer and track coach. He is a wonderful little man, and if I can get him interested in me I will be pretty sure to develop greatly in the next year.

Studies are getting more troublesome every day! Really it is terribly boring to sit indoors on these wonderful nights so crisp, cool, starry and lighted by the heavenly moon! In spite of them all I have been studying hard and feel as if I have covered a lot of ground. I *must* pass all my exams—then they will be dead and gone forever.

First, you were a peach to remember my natal day as you did! You know, I had completely forgotten that I was reaching my most mature age to date and it woke me up with a bump. I have been celebrating today by going to class, getting my laundry, and a shine downtown, and coming down to pay my respects to Prof and Mrs. Prof. I got here in time to wash the dishes (they have gone out to a dance or something) and shoo them out of the house and then my "literary art" began. Before that, however, I played on their piano and got real inspired. Somehow I didn't want to go just to the movies on my birthday—I can go to them any old time.

They had forgotten my birthday so when I came down tonight and they wanted to feed me, I put a match in a cruller and lit it. Then I told them it was my birthday cake.

They were sure surprised and invited me for dinner to-morrow. Wish I'd kept still!

You know your definition of a kiss? [1] Well, Girl, that little sentence won a high mark for me in my term's speech in Public Speaking! By George, Prof never laughs, and time after time I have gotten up and sat down again—failing to rouse him from his sternness. But on Thursday! The speech which *counts a third* of our term mark (the exam counts two-thirds) had to be given; I was desperate; I took an appropriate subject, "Large University or Small College" and worked that anecdote in as nicely as you please. The class roared and Illy—well, Illy just rolled around—and that means a darn good mark. No matter about the rest of it; I had a funny analogy and you helped me get a darn good laugh out of the most serious-appearing man in Lafayette College. Congratulations and thanks!

I am trying to decide whether to go out for track or for baseball. Darn it, you can't do both, and I'd like to try both. I have never tried running, yet the other day in gym period after all the stiff exercises we went out on the track and ran a half-mile. I came in fresh as a daisy and since then I have been trying every day for myself. My wind is about perfect (at last I am really glad that I don't smoke) and I don't break my stride. Wouldn't it be funny if after all this time of trying different things the one I have missed should prove the *real* one! I don't dare hope, and yet I think that I'll try.

[1] This definition was—"A kiss is an anatomical juxtaposition of two orbicular muscles in a state of contraction."

LARRY

Home Letter

You will be tickled to hear that I got Phi Beta Kappa grades. My average is just above the 4.5 standard of that honorary society. Three of us in the House rate Phi Bete, and all of the Frosh worked so well that our House is shoved way up in the scholastic standing higher than we have ever been before. 'Ray for the Frosh.

To Girl

Here is a sticker for you. You know how hard I worked in gym because I liked it; how I went out for basketball when I didn't have the ghost of a chance but thought that it was showing at least some class spirit; how I missed gym when I went out for basketball, thinking that I was excused (for one cannot do both). Well! I get an F in gym for the year. Flunk. Nice system, what? Think I'll see the dean this afternoon. Gosh, I was sore. I could have loafed all year and gotten an A or B by just *going* to gym and slipping by all the hard work.

Later.

It's afternoon now and I have just seen the dean. Yea for the home team! He said that basketball *is* recognized and that the Physical Director is batty; that I pass with flowing colors. Yea, again!

First you must know how glad I was and am and shall be that you were here. I was so afraid that something might happen to detain you or change your mind that when I saw you step off that train—well, I was relieved, if I may put it so mildly. What I really wanted to do was to rush up and grab you and yell: "Yea! Girl's here!" I was most awfully proud of you at the dances and things; and the fellows have been coming around saying that they thought I was a horrible pig to keep you to myself; that they wanted to meet you ever so much. Well, I *was* selfish.

The main trouble with most week-ends is that they have to bust off bang! like that. To ride home with you and talk our first real talk of the time, and just *see* you for so much longer, was the most wonderful way imaginable to end the little vacation.

Fearest Damily

Raise the flag and sound three long and incredulous cheers! I talked with Robert over a Welsh rarebit of our own making (thank goodness Selma didn't find us), and we decided that I could stay here four years and pass off the first two at R. P. I. If it is O.K. with you and if Rensselaer sends back a favorable reply to a letter which I shall send after I have your approval, everything will be set and I shall get the merry ha-ha from everyone who will say "I told you so. I knew when you got down there you wouldn't change." Well, so be it. Let 'em laugh. For the last few years laughing has been one thing I haven't minded.

To Girl

Here I am back to my old tricks; staying in Saturday night and writing you. There is a Damrosch concert and a debate and a few good movies, but I wanted to take life easy for a change and read Dickens. You know I'm getting positively fascinated with these real books. "When I'm an architect" I'm going to design houses—homes—with lovely big libraries and books reaching clear to the ceiling. And I'm going to live in one of those *homes* and spend lots of time reading in a deep lounging chair, with all the accompanying comforts such as slippers, grate fire, and maybe someone to read to. Coming under the head of comforts isn't exactly flattering, is it? But you know what I mean. By the way, read Stevenson's "Truth of Intercourse" from "Virginibus" again; it illustrates my case exactly in many instances: *not what I say, but what* YOU *know I mean,* is the way you should translate, or rather interpret, my speech and writing. If you can get hold of Lamb's "Old Familiar Faces," a short poem, read it. I'm crazy about the darn thing and it sure has a wonderful philosophy.

You know, for some reason or other I want to read to you and have you fool with my hair, all at once. Gee, it (meaning the hair) got cut today, and each one of the little dears was really sorry to leave me—it had been with me *so* long!

Tomorrow I'm going out with Joe and he says that I'm going to meet "one wonderful girl." There's one thing I've noticed about these "wonderful girls" I'm introduced to: they fall 'way short of a certain girl I know—but I'm from Missouri so I'm going tomorrow.

I nearly forgot to mention the "date" we made. Holy smoke, was it funny? I roar to think of the afternoon. Some day I must tell you every detail, but these are the glaring facts: Joe, Bob and I went to get the "wonderful" girls—

The swan dive
Camp Huntington, Mass.

Life-saving emblem won at
Camp Wawayanda, N. J.

and I nearly passed out cold when I saw them. Honestly I was ready for a good talk with a nice girl; beautiful day and I wanted to walk to Paxinosa. Well! This little prize is one of the horrible kind who think they're sophisticated. I have never in my life met *anyone* who knew so little about *anything*. Dumb, just absolutely, hopelessly, terribly dumb. Well, she and her friend were supposed to be quite the athletes at school, but they weren't walking ten minutes before they were "so tired" and "how much farther?" I wanted to push 'em off the cliff, but it would be hard on the people that found them, so I refrained.

Little Larry is getting to be a very busy child: he is in a *working* discussion group, and an Honor group that is trying to instil honor in the men of the freshman class. It is no easy job but we can try. Then I'm getting so fascinated with debating that I can scarcely wait until I have a chance on the platform.

I am out for track every day and in four years ought to be able to run around the house.

Now for the words of wisdom from Mr. Shakespeare through Polonius: "To thine own self be true." Girl, since I have come to college I have realized more and more the significance of those immortal words. We can do only our best wherever we are, and doing so don't need to worry about those things which we cannot do. "And it must follow as the night the day . . ."

This afternoon track was stiffer than it has been. Golly, we ran a mile and a quarter at three-quarters speed and little

Larry came in sadly blown and with throat of chalk. I had never run such a distance at such speed and I *was* tired. Then a nice cold shower and dress up for a walk downtown where I celebrated your birthday by getting the first sundae in months. I had just come back when Gebhardt, whom I have come to know rather well, called up and asked me to eat with him. We had a dandy meal and a finer talk about everything referring to college. He wants me to go to Clinton to speak to the Y.M. group there if possible.

The other night they had the banquet and instead of going I did something which I shall never be able to fully explain. I was at Illy's all afternoon working on my debate—otherwise I should have gone down for the riot part. Fully intending to go at six o'clock I picked up "The Plastic Age" and began to read. When I finished the last page it was way after six and I was sort of in a haze contemplating the whole matter. It had snowed heaps all day and something in me was revolted at the thought of the seething mob down at the Karldon. I wanted to think. Well, by golly, I was fool enough to stay right there and went out after dinner with Bob and Selma to shovel snow. Before I knew it I had cleared the path almost to the corner and I was soaked. Think? Say, I never worked my little think wheels so hard in my life. In other words, the "Plastic Age" is a lot truer than I would like to believe! Is that very shocking to you? I should believe so, yet that is my honest opinion. However, I know that only a small percentage of the men are typified by Hugh Carver. Percy Marks depicts the conditions which one meets—and he does it with remarkable skill and faithfulness. Where he is misleading is in the idea which one naturally gets that the *average* college man surrenders to the conditions. *That is not true.*

Enough about me and my crazy ideas. I would much rather talk of you but you seem so darn far away in terms of miles. On the other hand, you are very near to me and very helpful in deciding lots of things. If more of the men here at College had Girls rather than girls, there would be a great lessening of most College problems.

Whew! At last I can take a decent breath for half an hour—no! beg pardon, twenty minutes. Anyhow, last night we had our first practice debate with the affirmative and we won. Gosh, it's fun! Honestly I don't know when anything has given me such a thrill as to feel that I am controlling other people. Rebuttal work is sure amusing and I just piled on heaps of humor for the fun of it. At 4:15, which is fifteen minutes from now, I am going to practice in Pardee Hall with the coach and adjust my voice to a large auditorium.

I'll be in Ridgewood on Wednesday. Boy, I was never so anxious to get a vacation. I crave sleep and fun and 'ome and me mother. I sure am a spoiled child, but those things sound mighty good.

And now I'm home and believe me, it is very comfortable and restful after the mad rush. First I must tell you about the debate. We lost but it was because of something which we couldn't help and even the coach didn't feel very badly about it. We went down to Rutgers and Herb Brown and I were entertained at the chapter. Alec Ford and Mal Stron are Zetes there you know and they treated us royally in their very beautiful house. Then came the real time. Honestly, Girl, the thrill that I got out of that evening will be always an inspiration to me if I ever tire of talking. I felt that my words were actually controlling *men* and that they were bending to my will. Thrilling? Breath-takingly so! And Herb said that I would undoubtedly be on the 'varsity next year.

Today I go back. Naturally the days have flown by and there wasn't a chance in the world to catch them. I'm feeling so peppy and anxious to get back on the job that I know my vacation has been mighty successful in giving me rest and cream. You know I never appreciated cream until there was only milk to be had. From now on vacations will be days of cream for me. I've just loafed along so comfortably and easily and read "So Big" by Edna Ferber ('s darn good) and driven my fond mother around in the car. Oh, yes, and composed a theme of which Anthony is the subject.

"SMILIN' THROUGH"

Theme for English

"HE's *always* smiling! Doesn't the man have *any* troubles?"

How little they know him! Come from the south when a boy, this fine old negro has grown up amid the customs and environments of the north; has worked at every job from elevator boy to horse-wrangler; has been the loving father of

We had our step sing in front of Pardee. The whole college turns out and sings and the band plays, and somebody makes a speech, and everybody cheers and then we sing the Alma Mater, just when the birds are singing their evening song and the stars are beginning to pop out.

a very happy family; above all, has seen life in its entirety and has a very remarkable and livable philosophy: his smile. I believe it implicitly. When I look at him I forget his wide nostrils, his rich chocolate complexion; those fade away, and I see only his smile: humorous, whimsical, tender; the window through which the divine light of the man breaks and glows on all who come within range of his radiant personality. That smile is the transparent covering of his soul . . .

He is growing old now, but his philosophy will lighten the gloom of failing health and strength. Thank God for the faith and hope and love which I *know* exist when I see Anthony smile!

To Girl

Percy Marks talked at Vespers last night. He's extremely entertaining and earnest about college men and women. He said that people have received his book in the wrong spirit; that they have read only the dirt and passed up the other parts; that he devotes all but four chapters to the best side of college life and when he does bring in the bad he contrasts the best with it. The climax of the book is reached when the men come out of a poker game and show an equal appreciation for the highest type of poetry. As I think over the book in this light I find that he is right. The conditions are absolutely true to type, but Hugh Carver was naturally not the average. Marks said lots of really good things and, while he omitted in both book and talk the chance which he might have taken and brought in the Christian attitude and ideals of the vast majority of students, he really gave much good advice. "Men don't go to college to learn how to make a living; they go to learn how to live!" "Happiness is the ultimate goal of every man and only as he learns to appreciate beauty, truth, understanding, and hunger for knowledge so that through them he reaches for happiness will he get the true worth out of college." In other words Marks said that Phi Betes don't get everything, athletes don't get everything; the man who has really derived the most from his college education has an insatiable hunger for knowledge and even after he has left college will continue to read and study and appreciate the finest things so that life is filled to overflowing. Oh, he told us lots of things we know, but he crystallized our thoughts and put them into words. I wish you could hear him.

It's fun to be back again and my work is going easier. The work is harder but I know how to go at it better than I did several months ago.

Saturday we lost a disheartening game with Gettysburg and then I went to supper with Gebhardt. I think I told you of him. Anyway we had a marvelous bull session, the two of us, over Cherrystones and strawberry shortcake, and our main topic of discussion was "necking." (Pardon the French, but—damn the word "necking.") He has formed an anti-necking society and after I kidded him and his honesty for a time I found that he was—and is—in earnest. In his work with High School kids he says it is the greatest problem he has. I wouldn't commit myself to join his darn club and told him that I didn't think there could be any set rule. He insisted that there must be and after I thought it all out I told him my formula (sounds bad) principle, which I wish

I had had when you were here. The next time I see you I have more darn things to tell you—and that formula is one of 'em. You see, a talk like that with an older man goes a long way towards clearing up your own ideas and making them articulate. He is a real sport and a fine friend and is extremely anxious to meet you, thereby showing his good sense.

I went to the movies—"No Mother to Guide Her" or something melodramatic like that—and laughed my head off in just the most tearful parts. Afterwards I had a long talk with George about everything in general and then to bed.

The days are divine. Honestly, no matter what beliefs I might have in regard to religion, a day like this proves to me that there is a God. The grass is a vivid green, shrubs are just bursting with yellow and red buds, trees have a downy yellow-green foliage as well as the darker and heavier emerald, the patches of shadow are so darkly contrasted with the bright background that everything stands out in bold relief. The ivies are making the buildings beautiful with their fine traceries and over the whole living, singing, growing earth there is a pale blue Maxfield Parrish sky. Gosh, beautiful? Heavenly! And some fellows walk to class looking down at their shoes and never a smile on their faces. Why the poor prunes, they're missing the most gorgeous picture ever painted.

Last Friday night we had our first step sing in front of Pardee. The whole college turns out and sings and the band plays, and somebody makes a speech, and everybody cheers, *and* then we sing the Alma Mater, just when the birds are singing *their* evening song and the stars are beginning to pop out. When we hummed the chorus through that dusky twilight everybody had a lump in his throat and we realized the true college spirit. Talk about the cribbing, the cutting, the drinking, the petting, but standing against that and far outweighing it all is the real, basic, fundamental, glorious college spirit. After all, that's what we'll remember when we get out. It is true college life.

I came home last night, changed into some old clothes, and went to look up Bill. He works in the library (working through college) and when it closed we took a walk up to Paxinosa. We talked about everything and everybody and discussed many problems of college life. It is the first time since I have been in college that I have really found a man who fits in the rôle of a friend and I hope that it may be a lasting friendship.

About twelve-thirty we went back to his boarding house and after we made some tea we sat talking some more, arguing about books and the contemporary poets over "shoo-fly" pie, crackers and jam. It was lots of fun and I like him immensely. After an evening with him you think about many things, have new and wider concepts of things, and feel that it has been well worth while.

FRIENDSHIP

Theme for English

THE night was clear and there was a touch of crispness in the air. The stars hung nearer and brighter than usual and their twinkling radiance suffused the world in a pale glow, throwing the features of my friend into sharp relief. We wandered on, each busy with his thoughts, yet conscious of the comradeship and security of the other's presence.

"Well, old man?" He linked his arm with mine.

Need we say more? A complete understanding renders words useless; words which so seldom can be depended upon to express our true feelings. A touch on the arm, a warm handclasp, a smile of appreciation, conveys a sentiment far more poignantly to a friend than do myriads of glowing words. *Friend*, remember, not acquaintance.

Friendships form an inestimable part of one's life. By them it is possible to soar to the pinnacle of success, or slip to the hungry abyss; good or bad, they largely determine the individual. What could be finer than the fellowship, the understanding, the unselfishness, the devotion, the *love* of a friend? Effeminate? No! Friendship is a strong, virile, all-powerful love; such a love that some two thousand years ago led to the sacrifice of a life which gave a new meaning to the word *friendship*. . . .

Dearest Mother:

Somehow when we poor little fellows are home and see our mothers every day of the year we almost get to take them for granted. But when a good many miles come between us we begin to appreciate how nice it is to have a mother, a safe sort of place to go when we want help. To remind all of us they have instituted Mother's Day and kids dress up in white carnations and mothers smile proudly at their little white hopefuls.

So, Mother, while this Sunday is a special day on the calendar; while I don't write to you as much as I might, and while I don't wear a white carnation every day, I think you know how much I love you all the time and every minute, and this Sunday is no more special than any other one in that respect. "Every day is Mother's Day for me."

Two weeks from Monday exams start. The events of the year are winding up and we are practically Sophomores now. We talk of how we will rush the frosh and it is all very funny. There is *such* a difference and change of attitude.

'By, folks and 'specially Mother this time. Remember that with all *my* faults I love you still, and I hope you have a lovely Mother's Day.

Well, I'm a sophomore! Ain't that grand? I've taken all my exams, passed all my exams, forgotten all my exams—and I'm a soph. Yea-a! Tomorrow night I go to a dance in Clinton and on Saturday I shall pack and come home. You see my schedule said that French comes next Wednesday, but I sneaked in with another section and took it yesterday afternoon. I've had seven exams in three and a half days—two a day! Whew!

FRESHMAN YEAR

INVENTORIES

Theme for English

At least once every year merchants take an inventory of their stock and compare the result with that of the preceding year. This gives them a definite check on their merchandise; they find what they have had, what they have, and most important, what they need. In the same way, it is usually a profitable and enlightening process for us to make a personal inventory: to find out our strength and our weakness, our impervious and our vulnerable spots, our affinities and our antipathies, our accomplishments and our dreams, our successes and our failures.

I am in perfect health; though I do not play on a team, I am always in training. But I have failed in that I have never made a representative sport. Mentally I have broadened and deepened; I am beginning to get a vague idea of "what it is all about." However, I am hopelessly ignorant of countless fine things. I have made a few fine friends and many acquaintances, and my old friends are finer and dearer than ever. I have some useless "stock" to scrap, and much new to add. Yes, my first term was wonderfully worth while, but what a tremendous chance for improvement!

LAFAYETTE COLLEGE

SOPHOMORE YEAR

Dearest Family,

Gee, it seems funny to be back and be Sophs. Jake and I are rooming together and already we have made a heap of a good-looking study out of the things at hand. Here's a picture of the study as it looks now.

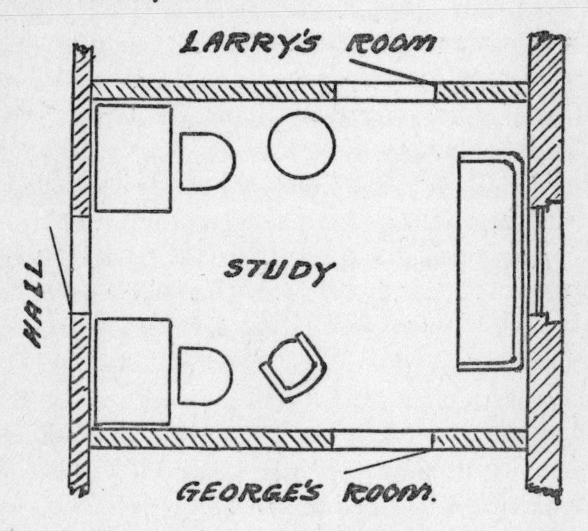

I wired a lamp and strung it across the room so that our desks are opposite. Now all we need are curtains for the study, lots of pillows for the lounge, three or four good pic-

Somehow this chapel gets me in a different way from
the awe-inspiring cathedrals of tremendous cities.
This one, ours, represents the new religion
corresponding to the new civilization

tures (no more banners and pennants for ours) and a bowl light, because we've decided on indirect lighting. There are no end to the possibilities of making it the best-looking suite in the House, and not a very expensive one either.

Do you remember the time I sold tags for the 4th and was tired of being polite? Well, it was nothing compared to this. All this week I've done nothing but smile sweetly at everyone and flatter them to death, *and* show them around. I almost say in my sleep: "Are you all fixed? Registered? Room and board? Fine! Now if there's anything I can do—. And you'll be down to lunch at the Zete House tomorrow? Fine! Yes, my name is Foster. Yes, 'F' like 'Fish'—" Ye gods! Jake and I went outside and called each other all the names we could think of—just for the mutual relaxation and affection.

I do wish that you might be here to see 'em all. They're *so* green! Almost as green as we were last year. Now *we* can say, *"HIT IT UP, FROSH!"*

I saw Selma and Bob this morning. She's very well and they are both crazy to get the baby. She is really going to be careful and not do too much. Getting sense at last, I told her.

To Girl

Oh, it's fun to be back and to know that this year things will begin to count. When I looked through the College calendar today I saw all the year's events behind me and myself a Junior. Then four years more—with what to look forward to? I get a thrill out of every little try that I make to see into the very exciting and elusive future.

LARRY

Sunday is such a nice day to see your friends and just take it easy and talk. That's the main reason why I don't do so many things on Sunday as a general thing. If I got into the habit I'd just race around the way I do the other six days and I feel that I need the relaxation and the enjoyment that comes from conversation and other people's society.

Yesterday we started our season by defeating Muhlenberg 13–0. Next week! Oh, the thrills that are running rampant around this campus! Next week we play Pittsburgh, and we'll play to win. It's our big game. Larry is going to bust his neck to get there if possible. Jake has a girl there so I can sympathize with his anxiety, but you see we can't find anyone to take us up and it's a heck of a long way. Just look on a map of Pennsylvania!

The work is going mighty well and I am getting organized. Classes are interesting and numerous; I'm on the go every minute and am enjoying myself immensely. Graphics especially is fun, like High School mechanical drawing only more so, and you know how much I love to fool with beautiful instruments. The Prof is a real man. English 3 is a survey course—Chaucer to modern times—and taught by one of the foremost doctors in the country, Tupper. Psyc—well, you know what psyc is!

Then the outside work is so much fun. I'm taking care of the frosh theme room (earning enough to come to you in November) and am getting to know Doc Tupper and lots of fellows. You knew that I was chosen for the Y Council? Well, at the first meeting Paul Lehman appointed me to the Cabinet as head of all the Personal Work for this year! It is a tremendous task; there is no end to the possibilities, but I am confident that I can do a really big piece of work. I wish that I could tell you all of my plans for vocational guidance, frosh council, foreign students, Cosmopolitan Club—concrete things that will not only strengthen the Y but definitely help the College.

I am also out for Glee and Instrumental Clubs and Debating is coming along soon. This is to be our biggest year and all of our old men are gone. Between you and me and the lamppost I'll have a good chance to make the 'varsity this year. Lafayette is getting interested in debating for Penn is now world champion and last year we beat Penn! If we can beat them this year do you know what it means? Trips all over the United States and to England as *World Champions!*

I took my physical exam and came out on top—one of the few who graded B or better. That gives me an optional choice of work and I shall take advanced gym. The equipment is so complete in the new gym that we'll never tire of it and it'll be a joy to work there.

Oh, I'm so excited about college that I can scarcely say enough! There is so much to do and so few who are doing it, it gives us poor dumbbells a chance.

Dearest Folks,

Today I passed another monthly quiz in Physics—and I would rather have taken physics than go to it too. But it wasn't so terrible. "The hills flatten out when you come to them."

Also I saw Tupper today and had a dandy chat with him.

LARRY

He wants me to write for the Tinsman Prize, a reward for the best yearly composition about a campus problem. I've been doing a lot of stray writing lately anyway, so I might just as well try for one hundred dollars as not, what?

I've traveled a long way since I last wrote you. Prepare to scold me for I bummed to Pittsburgh with Bill for the Pitt game! Gee, it was sure fun! Seven hundred miles since last Thursday.

Bill and I decided that we must see the game but we didn't want to spend all the money that it would cost, so at four forty-five in the afternoon we left and got a ride immediately. We got to Harrisburg at eleven and slept in the jail for want of a softer bed; not behind the bars, of course, but in a waiting room there. When we walked into the room and turned on a light we found eight other Lafayette men who had started before us. That floor was some hard!

We left about five-thirty and were very fortunate in getting some long lifts so that by five in the afternoon we were in Pittsburgh. Sleepy? Holy smoke, we could have shut our eyes and dropped off in a second.

We went to the big rally and pep smoker held every year by the alumni before the Pitt game. Then we stayed the next two nights at the Kappa Sig House—Bill's fraternity—and they treated us royally.

Of course you know that we won the game 10–0, and let me state that it was a corker—worth going seven hundred miles to see. We nearly went crazy because Pitt has a good team and is eight or nine times larger than we are.

I can't begin to tell you all the things we did and saw

and the people who gave us lifts. When I see you next I'll have a lot to tell you.

I learned all about a Ford car (patching up one of our "limousines"), have a thorough knowledge of the geography of central Pennsylvania, and an infinite respect for all truck drivers. I cultivated an enormous but perfectly reasonable appetite for it was a long way between meals more than once.

I spent $7—$2 for the game, $2.50 for a night in a Bedford hotel, and the rest for food. One of the other boys spent $28—$15 of which was mine!

MANIA

(After J. V. A. Weaver)

My God, Judge! Don't you think I got no feelin's?
Every day I drive that there truck
Haulin' sand,
Crawlin' along like I had four punctures
While little rattlin' Fords go whizzin' past,
And I go near crazy 'cause I can't just
Step on it, and go like hell!
Then some nights I gets the Chevvie
What belongs to my girl's Old Man,
And we goes skimmin' out by the park,
Flyin' along with the wind rushin' by,
Passin' other cars . . .
Speedin' was I? Well, who the hell
Wouldn't?

After supper last night the moon came up gloriously and I just couldn't go to the movies as I had planned, so I walked around awhile and then visited the new chaplain. He is Elliott Speer from New York—Dr. R. E. Speer's son. He's a prince and we bulled around for an hour and a half and then took both Mrs. Speer Junior and Senior out for a ride in his new car, and maybe it wasn't a beautiful ride!

He is a mighty fine fellow and tonight I am to have the honor of introducing Dr. R. E. Speer to the college at Vespers. Ain't I lucky?

ROADS

I took a long trip in an auto
And noticed several things about roads:
The best ones are those having good foundations
And good surfaces;
The rough stretches make you appreciate
The smooth ones;
The most interesting are those with many
Curves and hills;
The hills flatten out when you come to them;
But every good road leads somewhere . . .
I think that a life must be something like
A road.

Dearest Family,

Yesterday was the Pageant and from all reports it went off very well. I was in General Washington's army so I saw very little of it. You should have seen the old plugs we had to ride! When we pranced in somebody in the audience yelled, "Garbage today?" and the poor, broken things pricked up their ears and started going! Holy cat, it was awful!

Last night I took Betty to the Birth Night Ball and we had a wonderful time. We were in old-fashioned costumes and when we paraded in the Grand March under iridescent lights it was a beautiful sight.

Debate tryouts were held tonight and Larry as usual shot his little line without knowing how to even state the question. However, the judges smiled once or twice and I succeeded in arousing two of 'em from the coma they had slipped into, so it might have been worse, I guess.

This week-end I am on a Deputation team that goes to a county boys' conference in Frenchtown. I've been to conferences before, you know, but always on the *receiving* end. This time all is different; I am to lead meetings and give a sermon Sunday (imagine me preaching!) to say nothing of playing the fool and my banjo. Anyhow, I'll survive, even if the little white hopefuls don't.

We had a darn good time this week-end at Frenchtown, and while I would have given almost anything to have seen the W. & J. game and met Dad afterward, I feel that my time was even more profitably spent.

So while I went down there with a more or less condescending attitude, sort of feeling "Well, boys, it's a big honor for you to have me here," it wasn't long before I snapped out of it and realized very seriously that I was contributing nothing to them and they everything to me. Lord! the egotism of man! At least of this potential man. I'm sober now; I'm beginning to catch a glimpse of just the conditions existing among the boys of the country and the possible ways that these conditions may be met—*if we have the leaders*. Oh, yes, I may be a "Y" secretary! Hot dog, ain't I got the definite plans for the future though?

I met some mighty fine people in that little one-horse town. You probably don't know that only eleven hundred people live there; that they make spark plugs, raise chickens, and gossip about a new recipe and a new courtin' with equal relish and facility—and imagination. So one hundred live kids with natural enthusiasm and energy more or less stirred up the place and they treated us royally. Good, homely, common folk, honest and hard working; the kind that keep alive one's faith in the good old American stock—these were our hosts. I was in one family, two adorable kids and very sensible parents who would do anything to make you comfortable. So you see I went down there and *got* everything for Larry; and I'm ashamed of myself that I didn't give more.

I nearly forgot to tell you that I made the Debating Squad. I near passed out I was so happy. Herb Brown talks as if he is going to give me a chance some day soon. All I ask is *one* chance.[1]

[1] Herb Brown, the debating coach, wrote in his diary concerning Larry's work on the Debating Team: "I am happy Larry made the 'varsity debate team. He always brings to his work a spontaneous enthusiasm and a challenging mind that will make work with him a sheer joy . . . and it should do a good bit to bring debating back to its rightful place here at Lafayette. The moment the campus sees that debating attracts men who are also able to do something else besides talk, there will be more support for the men on the teams. Larry is the best possible recommendation for intercollegiate debating."

To Girl

Everything now is preparation for our first debate. Last night they had a practice debate between our own teams. I was all confident; thought I was the whole cheese. Herb Brown gave me the first negative speech and the last rebuttal—positions of honor—and I swelled two more inches. Then I got to the platform—and (to be perfectly frank) forgot every damn thing. I saw words on my notes and I had a vague knowledge that they were waiting for me to say something; and I flunked out cold. Don't know why; I wasn't scared; only our own teams were there—no judges. I just couldn't function. I sat down.

Herb gave me my rebuttal to see if I could redeem myself and I came through fairly well but didn't have any snap. I lost my confidence. So did Herb.

Since then I have had a long session with Herb. My confidence has come back—so has his. You can be very sure that Larry will work his fool head off this week because I must reinstate myself with the team next Tuesday night. My speech is in outline form and I promise you that it'll be a corker.

You still don't see what I mean about a boy having a girl for an ideal. I don't mean that the girl must be ideal—"they ain't no sich animal, I guess." But the boy can live so that he will be more worthy of the best that is in him—and this "best" is always what he thinks the girl would have him be. The girl is his standard—his ideal. He thinks "What would she think of me if I did this?" or "What would she want me to do now?"

LARRY

Dearest Family,

Glee and Choir practices were held this afternoon and I sure enjoy singing. We have our first concert in Easton on December 3rd and we're all set to knock 'em dead. And this week Sunday in chapel the choir will sing for the first time and I sure hope that we get away with it. We were selected from the College so we don't *dare* flunk the singing!

Last Wednesday I stopped in to see Selma and that sweet lady was almost in tears. She had had a mean cold and was feeling rotten in general so I stayed without being invited, had a good dinner, washed the dishes, and stayed long enough to cheer her up a bit. She's pretty large now and finds it difficult to tear around much. She's a peach; I'm crazy about her. She showed me all the baby things and I'm tickled to death that I'm to be an uncle—or aunt.

Gosh, that was a nice thing for Dad to do—send me a special delivery letter before the debate. It just put me at top-notch. Believe me, that letter burned a hole in my pocket when we knew that we had lost. For that's what happened. I can't realize it yet because we were so *sure* we had won! Golly, I would have bet all the money I'll ever make that we had won. But evidently the judges disagreed with us. Anyway it was a good debate. We fought every minute and we gave those boys an awful battle. So I have no regrets at all, except that I'm sick for Herb's sake—we did want so much to win for him.

So, mine folks, endeth a very unfortunate week-end as far

as votes went, but I am even more in love with debating than ever. Just wait 'til next time! [1]

To Girl

Our Open Forum Club is starting tomorrow night, led by Prof Steever, one of the best of the whole faculty, and we're going to have a darn good group this year, I'm sure. We discuss everything from college dances to the immigration question, and while it is subject to more or less supervision by a Prof it is very natural and spontaneous—as it should be—but very instructive also. It really makes college worth while to know men who are willing to get to the bottom of things with you. We have lots of fun cussing and discussing.

This is our initiation week and we are naturally making up for last year. About twelve o'clock last night the poor devils were hauled out of warm beds, bundled up to the ears, blindfolded, and then given nice, long rides—free of charge. I went with Bob, Hart and Kearny and we sure took the boys on a lovely airing in the most dismal neck of

[1] To quote again from the coach's diary: "This evening at the House Larry Foster and I held a post-mortem on the surprising result of the debate at Lancaster. Larry told the story with mournful voice and laughing eyes—'Heck, Herb, we convinced the audience and the other team—in fact everybody but two pesky judges. We did our darndest, and it was much better than the trial contest last week; in fact, you would have been tickled to death at the work of the other two men. Bob and Clarence were simply great and in the rebuttal I thought they left nothing for the other side to rest its case upon.' That satisfied me and it is just like Larry to talk of the work of the 'other fellows' without a word about his own part. And then, to cap it all, Larry smiled at Jake, who was in the room, and wound up with a tremendous 'and we are ready for victories in every debate left on the schedule!' "

the woods that ever you saw. There wasn't a house for miles, the roads were continually branching and running in the opposite directions, the sign posts were rotten to illegibility, and altogether the prospects for a speedy return to those warm beds must have seemed mighty slim. Of course they weren't very far from home—only about eight or ten miles—but we hoped that they would get lost, and that's exactly what they did. It may sound heartless as the very dickens, but it does some of these men an awful lot of good and it always shows up the real worth of a man.

I wrote a theme on my initiation last year that described my own sensations.

BLIGHTED HOPES

Theme for English

PHYSICIANS say that the hour between three and four o'clock in the morning is the time when vitality is at its lowest point. Certainly this was so in my case one night last December. I had been walking since midnight, at first with brisk strides and then, as the road unwound before me like a satin ribbon in the moonlight, at a more moderate pace so that my energy might last until my destination—how far away I did not know—should be reached. I watched the dismal moon drift across the uncertain sky only to be blotted out by black cotton-batting clouds which scudded before a rising northwest wind. The cold became more intense and so easily pierced my light costume that at times I had to run to keep warm. The night got inky black and heavy gusts swept against my chilled body. Home was very far away and a bed an unattainable luxury. Mechanically I plodded on and on until the lights of an auto appeared suddenly behind me and transformed the road into bright ridges and black valleys, stretching into space. . . . The auto would stop and pick me up and I would have rest, and sleep comfortably, warmly, divinely! Sleep, rest. . . . The auto sped nearer and nearer —I waved my arms—and the throttle opened with a roar as the car thundered past me into the night.

But to get back to this year, I almost lost an eye when we were riding around last night, it was so darn beautiful. Cold and clear, and light as day under that fiendish, freezing moon! Brrr! I was glad that I was not the little feller that had to drift around all night carrying all sorts of crazy bundles, making it absolutely necessary that one's hands get nice and congealed. And today is the perfect sequel to that night. Clear and blue, much scudding clouds that play hide and seek with the sun, and a mean north wind that drones softly in your ear until you're off your guard—and then swells into a wild shriek, snatching your one and only hat and sending it whirling off across the quadrangle. I don't dare go up to Paxinosa—I might blow off.

This morning in Chapel we heard one of the best speakers to college men in the country: Dean Brown of Yale. Without any exception he is my idea of the perfect public speaker —clear, forceful, direct, homely; above all, having something to say. Gosh, and he does say it, too! I'm going over to the Cantata now; be back later to tell you all about it.

Later.

The Cantata was excellent. A choir from town came up to the college and sang Nevin's new composition, "The Incarnation," and they sang it remarkably well. I was especially crazy about the soprano; she just tore 'way up the scale as lightly as a flute. Nevin is a graduate of Lafayette and lives in Easton. Last year he wrote "The Crucified" which I like even better than I do this new one. We stayed for the Communion that they have every year before Christmas, and truly I love to go to it! One has the feeling that it is at such gatherings of the men that the real spirit and worth of the college comes to the fore. In spite of the conditions which exist in the colleges, in spite of the fact that men profess to ignore religion, I know that underneath it all is the deep-seated reliance on Someone or Something greater. There are numberless creeds and beliefs among the fellows—all types and kinds of denominations—but no matter what Deity they believe in the fact remains that they do believe, and it is at a Communion service of the kind we have here that the men show themselves in their true light—bless 'em!

But then, you probably know me for what I am—just a foolish sentimentalist! Somehow that Chapel gets me in a different way from the awe-inspiring cathedrals of tremendous cities. This one, ours, represents the new religion corresponding to the new civilization, in contrast to the superstition corresponding to the Old World. Ours is bright and airy; theirs was dark and gloomy. We hear from the greatest Minds and Hearts of the time; they burned incense and worshipped traditions. We receive inspiration to live finer lives; they indulged in their superstitions.

Our initiation will probably keep going until this coming Thursday. It's deadly tiring for us and it's hellish suspense for the Frosh, but when we start to put the pledge buttons aside for the pins—oh, then, everything will have been worth while! It sure is a grand and glorious feeling; they tell me that the only feeling that approaches it is the time that a certain ceremony is mumbled over a ring.

I hope that the folks can come for me in the car this Friday. If it's decent weather the chances are pretty good, but if it snows like the deuce—Larry'll walk. You see I told you that I bought the "pay-rents" Christmas presents and I'm flatter than a sheet of paper—blank.

I can't help thinking of the contrast between this week-end and the one that might have been had I not turned the situation over to Larry. You see, he's a frivolous sort of boy, not a brain in his head, and a horrible example of the present day and generation. But he has one virtue: a love of fun. This week-end proves it conclusively, because he's had a wonderful time and you've been adorable to him every minute. But there is one big trouble with Larry—that is, one very serious trouble: one is liable to get the idea that he is all fun, that because he is a good dancer as you say he is, he could dance well in business; that because he has responsibilities in college and meets them as well as he can, he could handle the far greater responsibilities in life. Not even he is sure of himself there. In other words, the "Larimore" part is so much bunk and the poor boob Larry is all that is left.

He is very crazy about you. He knows that you are the very finest girl he has ever met, that it is mostly you who keep him doing the things he tries to do. But he is getting afraid that you see him only at the times when he is Larry; that because he does dance and play and talk once in a while you will forget that he really is a dumb nitwit who has never proved anything—to say nothing of himself!

Please be lenient with him! He will make loads of mistakes and you will be madder than a hatter at the remarkably foolish stunts that he will pull off in the next few years. But there are hopes for him and if you stick with him he'll have a much easier time—because it gets pretty darn hard sometimes. All this is so you will know a bit more of him—of the part of him that few see. Please accept this note of explanation from the

Boy.

By all means see the eclipse of the sun. There's an egotist for you; only entirely covers his face once in four hundred years!

Dearest Mother,

Your son wants to wish you a happy birthday. In spite of the fact that grown-ups from the appalling age of thirty on hate like the deuce to tell their ages (and this type is usually the kind that get their faces "taken up" much like the reefs in their souls), I am taking this natal day of yours as a chance to say that the only difference your age makes to me is that you're sweeter every year. And, gosh, that is getting to be so sugary that I'll have to suck a lemon before I kiss you—to counteract the sweetness!

I like you to be over fifty! You have a certain prestige that a person of forty-eight can't possibly have; why, you can say "damn," just like that, and it sounds infinitely better than someone else saying "how disagreeable!" And you command just the right amount of respect. It's the most natural thing in the world to see men and women alike rise when you enter the room. Yet they're not afraid of you—not judging from that awesome epithet and caress, "Aunt Molly!"

But you seem as if you are only about twenty, too. Somehow you understand things so nicely—especially things about your son. And I'm the only son you ever had, by George, so you haven't had an awful lot of practice—only nineteen years. But you know all the things that you should and shouldn't about me without my saying a darn thing; I've started to tell you loads of confessions—and then seen in your eyes that you knew 'em all the time. What's a fellow to do but adore you? You have such a big advantage—you don't give him a chance!

Yes, ma'am! If being fifty-six means that one can be loved and respected as you are, be as attractive as you are, be "Aunt Molly" to a flock of nieces as you are—and yet be Dad's girl sweetheart and my best girl, as you are—then may old Time do his stuff in making as many people as possible fifty-six in as short a fifty-six years as possible. Certainly it is an age to be envied of the gods!

And, Mom, you know me well enough to understand that all of this has been scribbled down because I love you. Not that I wouldn't believe it otherwise—for I can't conceive of anyone knowing you without loving you—but the only proof that I can give is that if for no other reason, I should always give the very best of myself for you. Happy birthday, dear.

To Girl

Hang it, I'm pepped up as the deuce tonight—have been all day. I went to fencing with just enough foolhardiness and devil-may-care attitude to disconcert the others and I eliminated a few more in the class. Of course we are not having formal bouts but I am fencing with all of the pupils so that I'll be able to count on the ones I can defeat. You know I'm all wound up about this darn sport; it's the thing I've been waiting for all my life, I guess. I'm narrow and consequently hard to stick; I have a long reach and can lead 'em on, ending up with a touch on a quick thrust; I'm in excellent training all the time, of course, and so have more endurance than a lot of fellows. Thank the Lord that I've not been smoking or drinking. Coördination is *so* vital—oh, I guess there's something to be said for keeping in training and condition after all.

But there's something so dashing and suggestive about it all; you can so easily believe that you're saving your hide and protecting the honor of the Head of the House and capturing the beautiful princess—oh, heck! you know how I *would* feel about it. And I really believe that I've found something that I can do! A long cheer for the home team!

Dearest Folks,

Truly there isn't much to tell of. Exams start next Wednesday and if all goes well I'll be home a week later for four days. Except for my full afternoons, fencing classes, Y.M. Council discussions (they've been hot!), cabinet confabs, committee meetings, Open Forum Club, and a new job they've wished on me—a literary society!—I haven't been doing very much. I'm in top notch condition and rarin' to go!

To Girl

To begin with, what have you been reading? Did I tell you that I've finished the "White Monkey" and Morley's "Haunted Bookshop"? Very likely, I was quite gone on both of them. My latest conquest is Benson's "From a College Window," which all well-educated young people are supposed to have read, so I shall not ask you if you have perused its musty pages. Rather an interesting collection of essays on all sorts of subjects.

In the Y.M. Council meeting a week ago there was a rumpus raised because someone suggested that the Y start a literary club. Right away another sap said that it wasn't the province of the Y to do anything of the kind; that if we wanted to save souls and play goody-goody that was one thing, but it was ridiculous that the Y should know anything about literary things. Well, you can imagine what I wanted to tell that man! Anyhow, I kept still for a change (I've been talking too much lately so I'm swearing in a new policy) and left it to be refuted by someone else. It was. Mr. Vogler is an all-round good fellow in spite of the fact that he's a Y secretary, and it was like waving a red flag in front of a bull to say such a thing before him. He lit into this boy—justifiably you will admit—and then there was a row. Anyway, I was appointed to a committee to look into the matter—no one else would take the job!

Thursday night the flare-up was due for another set, so everybody expected including Larry, but I had worked the thing out as well as I could and the other boys agreed, and after the other work was out of the way there was an ominous silence and my report was called for. As usual the squabble was settled as soon as the facts were known. I said that we agreed that a literary club was needed. That was one thing we were sure of. Then another was this: that up to the present no one has had the initiative to start such a club. Granted again. Now, I hold that the true function of the Y is to be of service to the men; that if they need something that can be done we'll do it, and let who wants to take the credit, so I suggested that a committee that understands something of the present conditions and the possible remedy for them be appointed with the definite idea of starting a club—a nucleus at first of reliable men—and gradually enlarging it until it fulfills the prominent place on the campus that it deserves. And the main point is that it doesn't matter a tinker's damn who starts the thing or pulls the glory of it as long as it is started, and started well.

By heck, you should have seen the faces of the radicals who had come for blood! You see they expected that the Y would run everything from formal parliamentary law to religious discussions, and when they found that the Y would do the thing as they wanted but take all the work away from them, giving them the fun of the thing, why, they just collapsed. And the screaming thing was this: the senior who has

Brainerd Hall, the "Y" at Lafayette College

"I hold that the true function of the Y is
to be of service to the men; that if they
need something that can be done
we'll do it, and let who
wants to take the credit."

been causing all the trouble (the kind who is hurt because his advice isn't consulted), and who has been damning the Y in general and Larry in particular; was so unnerved that he rose and moved that the same committee be continued, myself as chairman, to work the matter out.

This morning Bill and I went over to the Grace Reformed Church where we are going to take a Sunday-school class between us; when he's here and I'm here we'll take different classes, but should one of us be away the other will fill in. And even if we don't do everything according to Hoyle (or Foster), at least the kids will have someone older there who hasn't had the chance and experience to ossify.

Poor little devils, they know more about football than any of the decent things that kids ought to know about. This morning I didn't have any idea of what type of studying they had had (I know now that they haven't had any) so I told them about the physical Christ; you know, the kind of story that would appeal to husky little brats from the seventh grade —played up the beauty of a wonderful body and how Jesus was the perfect example. Gosh, I was afraid that I'd overdone it and that they might want to know if He played on the All-Israel Team! But they got it, and I honestly think that it was the first time they had ever had an idea along that line; most of them admitted that they had thought of Christ as a mollycoddle and teacher's pet!

Dearest Family,

I had a lovely birthday. Girl sent me a handkerchief that she made—gosh, it must have taken a month!—and it's darn good-looking. Then Monday night I took George and Bob to Grand Opera; the first I've seen. The New York Opera Company put on "Il Pagliacci" and "Cavalleria Rusticana," and they were darn good. Of course as long as I don't know anything about it they may have been awful, but ignorance was bliss in this case—I enjoyed it hugely.

Nothing has happened since. I've taken my two easiest exams and passed 'em. However, I did see the Illys "at home" with Carol.[1] Gee, it's funny! Selma a mother! She's a peach. They're all well and happier than they can say in spite of midnight séances and afternoon squallings.

To Girl

If I were a girl and wanted to vamp a man I'd arrange for somebody to poke him one on the head and raise a good bump, feed him something to give him indigestion and then let him stay alone all evening with only pessimistic books to read. Then at about ten-thirty, when he begins pacing the floor, blow in in all my glory and soothe his aching dome. Hot dog! If he wouldn't come around—well I wouldn't *want* him for a husband!

Note that I am home. Gosh, it feels good to just amble around, stretch myself luxuriously in a dressing gown and slippers, read or play the piano whenever I want, snag a piece of cake when I begin to run down, and in general thumb my nose at the clock. But I've said before that I'm a lazy little feller; this is simply further proof. Not that *you* need it!

[1] Carol was a professor's new baby.

I passed all of my exams and that means that I have only a year and then another year, and then a half-year—and then what? By that time I'll be twenty-one and maybe a *great big man.* Why gosh! I'll be able to vote and stay out after twelve o'clock at night! My nineteen-year-old responsibilities are weighing on me heavily now. What'll they be in two more years?

Yesterday I fussed around with books all morning. That pile I bought at Christmas has come and I've been so tickled that I've arranged them forty different ways—first according to size, then authors, then importance, and then back again. But it's a good list and the ten Dickens books look good enough to eat. "David Copperfield" goes back to Easton with me.

Dearest Folks,

I'm sorry that I didn't write last week but I have been on a nice trip. You have heard of the Student Volunteer Movement probably; I was chosen to go with some others to represent the college, and we had lots of fun. The true purpose of the convention was to get men and women to become missionaries and train for that as a life work. I do not expect to do that of course, but it was a good chance to get away and have some fun, and anyway I wanted to know what it was all about. So George and I from our house, and four others, went to Lancaster, Pennsylvania, and there was the dumbest conference that I have ever seen. I was disappointed in the type of men and women who are going out in Christian service. If I were a heathen I would be hard to convert, believe me. But the trip was worth while because I met the

Hon. A. B. Hess and his lovely wife. George and I stayed at their home and I'm telling you I shall count them as among my finest friends all my life. My estimation of the Pennsylvania Dutch and the Mennonites has gone way up.

To Girl

Robert has gone home to see his mother and I am staying with Selma until Monday night. We're having loads of fun even if I am scared to death that the fire will go out any minute and freeze the baby! But we'll get along all right. I'm trying to do as much to relieve Selma as I can because a three-weeks-old baby requires a heck of a lot of attention, doesn't it? At least I can do all the work without telling her how to raise her baby properly. I'm tickled to pieces that I can do it for them and so pay 'em back in a small measure for what they've done for me.

Carol is a dear. She sleeps like a trooper all the time and has used her lungs so seldom that I'm scared to death she'll be hollow-chested, although from the models that I've seen demonstrating the débutante slouch she'll be right in style, I guess. You know I'm so glad that you are different. I'm glad that you walk as if you knew where you're going; I'm glad that you don't have to resort to cigarettes for popularity; I'm glad that you look people in the eye; I'm glad that your color comes from the inside rather than from a box; I'm glad that your mind is used for thinking. Oh! I'm glad that you are *you!* Honestly, when I see the troop of females who grace our schools and colleges I wonder just what the next forty years is going to be like. And when I see the damn-foolishness of the men of the colleges—whew! I grow rabid. Oh, I love all that you stand for; that you are! I hope I can be just a bit more worthy of knowing you at all! Take care of yourself; have just the finest kind of time, and once in a while—write!

The fates are doing me dirt as far as seeing you is concerned. I can't come! Oh! I *can't* come. Honestly, it's so darn rotten, but I have at least four important meetings to attend—not the ordinary kind but the kind that demand my presence because you see I called all of them, started them, and I *have* to be there! I've raved so much about responsibility that I simply must live up to my own preaching now, and if I missed this week-end I wouldn't have the face to say anything again. You see, don't you? Oh, if it were anything that I could give up myself or change around to suit, but I *can't*. I hope you can get someone else to play with you (I love to have you call me "first fiddle"), but I'll be miserable this week-end when I think of what I'll be missing.

Dearest Family,

Well, I'm here! After swearing that I wouldn't come! I'm an awful nut. You see Girl wrote Tuesday asking me—apologizing for the late date and everything—and I sent back a stricken letter (you know) saying that I had too much to do over the week-end, four meetings and all that sort of thing. And I called myself names for the next day or two for not accepting. Then one of the meetings—the most important one—was called off, and I thought, "Well, what the—! Everyone else is canceling meetings for his own pleasure, so Larry will also." And he did, and sent a wire pronto, and here I am.

I bought a fur coat the other day—the goatskin one—for $39.50, and the fellows are crazy about it. But you'd die laughing to see me parading around in it here. I forgot that only at college were they known and that the people of New York and New London wouldn't savvy at all. I sure did get a razzing in New York yesterday, and if I passed two thousand people on the street, one thousand nine hundred and ninety-nine turned around to glare at me. "My dear, look at that"; "Ain't it swell, huh?"; "Bearskin—"; "Polar bear, I'll bet"; "Cost a thousand if it cost a—"; "Damn teddy bear"; "The way these college boys spend their—"; "Holy smoke, look at that!", etc., etc. These are merely samples, but it sure is a scream. If they only knew I paid $39.50 for it!

I'm just on my way back to college from New London and have to wait two hours in New York. I would like to call you up but am afraid to disturb you at this ungodly hour so will write instead.

Oh, but we had a "scrumptious" time! Honestly, from the time I got there until I *had* to come away the minutes flew by with no earthly excuse, except that I must leave eventually and they seemed to hurry my departure.

Friday night Girl and I talked until the dreadful hour of ten-twenty (when all the little girls must be in bed) and then we got some wonderful sleep. Yesterday I bummed around and saw the sights until Girl had finished classes and then we went to the Tea House for lunch. Girl played on the sophomore hockey team and they won the game with the juniors so we all enjoyed that part of the afternoon. Then there was a little tea-dance (and they really served *tea!*) and we stayed only long enough to get warmed up before we went downtown to the Huguenot, the little waffle place that I liked so much when I was there last year. Then the big formal at night and oh, but it was fun. Girl looked adorable as usual and the gym was very attractively decorated. Of course the music was perfect and I had all the best dancers on my program due to Girl's engineering, so *that* part of it was marvelous. By the time we reached Thames Hall where Girl lives she had to be in and I came home for another lovely sleep.

This morning we went for a peach of a horseback ride way back in the woods where the college has a hut for the Y.W. The surroundings are lovely and we had lots of fun crashing through the branches on our fiery steeds. Then we ate and took a walk—and it was time for me to leave.

It was a wonderful week-end. We both wanted you there *so* much.

To Girl

I must tell you of my funny trip back. Before I've always sat in the coach and gotten the onions and garlic and fish, so I had the sudden inspiration to sit in the smoker. Well, the first half hour was not so bad; I was dozing and sort of dreaming around about all the things that had happened during the week-end, and all of a sudden I woke up feeling as if someone were choking me. It was the car! Ye gods, what a stench! You could cut the blue haze with a knife and it wasn't made with fifty-cent cigars, either. I lit out and nursed a headache for the next two hours. I thought I could stand lots of tobacco smoke but I'm licked. I admit it.

Before we pulled into New Haven I picked out a fairly clean-looking individual in the coach and sat next to him. He left at New Haven and a very nice gentleman parked beside me, offered me his paper, used my suitcase for a foot rest, and immediately began reading a manuscript. From my poor vantage point I nearly broke my neck trying to read it and the little I saw was very dull and uninteresting—everything described in detail and the present tense. I came to the conclusion that he was writing nursery rhymes.

But my friend didn't want to read long because he had a cold in his eye, and as I looked very attentive and promised to be a good listener he started going. He was very interesting and I was sorry to leave him in New York. He is a Mr. Hender from Astoria who has been an actor of some note but now is the research director of Famous Players, and I was all ears as he told me of the big plays and the tiny details in 'em. It was fascinating and I learned more about the inside workings in the two hours with him than I would the rest of my life, I suppose. He told me about "Janice Meredith" and many of the troubles they had with the production purely because of fake thoughts on history and poor interpretations of it. He sure is up on the lives of great men.

Well, I had two hours to spend in New York before my train left for Easton so I took my time and walked to the Pennsylvania Station. A very well-dressed man in evening clothes came up to me and said, "Pardon me, but would you mind telling me what kind of fur that coat is made of?" I looked him very gravely in the eye and said, "My dear sir, it will give me very great pleasure to inform you as to the character of this masterpiece. This creation may rightfully be called the triumph of the goat!" Well, he thought I was cracked. He stopped right still in the middle of the street and three taxis almost clipped him—at least I didn't see him again.

I made an outline of the essay that I want to write and still had three-quarters of an hour to spend so I walked some more and watched the bright lights for a while. Broadway is fascinating when you've plenty of time to appreciate it. By one o'clock I was so sleepy that it's a wonder I got the right train. I fell asleep before we were out of the station and woke up just as we were pulling into Easton with a stiff neck and a broken arm and the knowledge that I had been lying on my one and only hat.

AT THE PENN STATION

Theme for English

It is twelve o'clock in the Penn Station and I am leaning against the base of a great Corinthian column. As I look along the shaft up to the capital it seems to be reaching toward the vaulted dome bending above; with all its grace and beauty it is struggling; upward. . . .

I have just come away from the lunch counter. When I

paid my check and reached for the change I thanked the clerk and smiled. His rather pitiful answering smile had a hard time to break the weary lines of his face; not many people thank him and smile, and he is tired.

Two painted things are passing me. They are laughing loudly and flirting with their escorts, but both have deep lines under their eyes and drooping from their mouths. The smiles are made of rouge, and their laughter comes back to me hollow and harsh (apparently life gave them nothing and they are out to see what they can get).

A drunk comes along. Helpless, hopeless, he has no control over mind or body, he has lost his self-respect, his honor, everything; his face is best witness to that. He staggers, stumbles past me and careens across the great room; another member in the ever-changing crowd. He will stumble and stagger through life, never finding himself, never finding *anything* worth while.

Here comes a porter. "Carry your baggage, boss?" He hasn't much to do but he is doing it well; he is contented with his small part because he doesn't think of a larger one. He is fed, clothed, busy and therefore has no worry. His grinning face fades away in the crowd, brilliant teeth shining from their ebony setting in a happy smile. Someone tipped him a dime.

A business man apologized for bumping into me. Head lowered a trifle, he is going his way feeling the heavy burden of responsibility. Prosperous family man though he is, he is wishing that business took a smaller part of life; that he might get home with the wife and kids more often; he realizes that he has taken his work too seriously. Now it is too late—he has no one to whom he can shift the weight. He has always wanted to do the work himself—resolutely he squares his shoulders and enters the subway.

A young bride and groom go by me, arm in arm. They look at each other and laugh, a deep, happy laugh that comes from 'way inside; their eyes are tender, their hearts are light, their steps are springy. As he passes me he looks up—and a sudden seriousness changes his fine face for a moment. He must reach up, up! It is a struggle! Then his hand tightens on her arm and he laughs again, confidently; they will climb together.

After all the columns express my feelings best. They are the true successes in architecture. Some people have the pedestal, the foundations, and lack the finish, the beauty of reaching the heights; some reach for years and find foundations crumbling; some never start; others too late; some build slowly and well, climbing and straining and attaining the upper crags of the world. Their life is best. They have beauty and strength; theirs is the grace and power of struggle and reward; they have climbed and won; they carry the load of their responsibility on competent shoulders; they are making the finer and more beautiful world!

To Girl

The Glee Club left Easton Thursday morning and broadcasted from WOR at Newark at two-thirty in the afternoon. We had more darn fun that can't all be told in a letter necessarily limited to three dozen pages, and I got to know and like very much the personnel of the Glee Club.

We took the two o'clock train for Patchogue, Long Island,

and got there about four-thirty. Four of us were put with the Robinsons, a wonderful family living in a lovely old colonial house on the turnpike near town. Well, that family treated us royally—honestly there was *nothing* they didn't do for us. It was because of them that I could carry out a brilliant idea I had. You see, the one criticism I (and I'm not alone) make about us is that we're too formal—we sing like so much Orpheus Club and you'd never know it was a bunch of college men *at all*. People go to a college glee-club concert to hear a little bit of college, remind them of days they were there, etc. As proof of it, our quartet has one or two comedy numbers that are welcomed uproariously after so much serious stuff. *Well*—the idea was to liven the thing up a bit, and it *sure* did.

I wandered out to the Robinson barn and got a great big squashy *rotten* cabbage; then Joe wandered me downtown in the car and I made up a list of certain delectable vegetables; then to the florists for some asparagus fern and green paper —and I began my bouquet—

The quartet was just starting another number when Bill stepped on the platform and began, "Ladies and gen—" They thought he'd gone batty and motioned to him to get the deuce off the stage. He smiled and went right ahead—thanked the four men for their commendable work and wanted to present as a token of our appreciation and esteem— Here Oscar and myself came gravely down the aisle holding my bouquet at a suitable distance, and Bill presented the thing to poor Forrest, the leader. In his nervousness he hugged the smelly thing to his manly bosom—thereby ruining one tuck shirt. But he was a good sport; he made some clever crack and the quartet rallied bravely, but the audience—well, say, the audience just *rolled* around hanging on to their sides! It doesn't sound so funny when I write it, but if you could have seen the expressions on the men's faces! From then on, the place was entirely ours, the bunch would clap before we started to sing and almost before we'd finished—they were *most* enthusiastic. And as a result the club was excellent; *really* excellent. The very best work I've heard. But Bill and Oscar and I stayed away from the quartet for an hour. Discretion of course.

Did I tell you that Betty took me to the Orpheum to the Easton Symphony Tuesday? Well, someone gave her tickets at the last minute and so she called me up and asked me. I decided quickly; I wanted to know her and I wanted very much to hear the orchestra. So we went—and I liked both. She's a darn nice girl and you know how few "darn nice girls" there are. She works in a law office downtown and apparently has been too busy to pick up all of the foolishness that the less industrious have. She is over twenty, I suppose, rather a nice kind of girl to know when one is in college, 'cause she's sensible and attractive—a happy combination.

Because of very good times on very good trips around the 13th and 20th of this month I pulled two beautiful marks: D in English and a straight flunk in History. Mean student, huh? But one can bring up marks while one cannot make up for lack of friends. I feel that both trips were wonderful for me. Such acquisitions cannot be tossed aside for two marks, but I will try to get both in future.

"The fear that keeps men little is the fear of being great!"

Good, isn't it? I heard it at the play this week and I want to remember it.

Dearest Family,

I am pledged Tau Kappa Alpha! You know it is considered everywhere *the* honorary society. While it isn't as universal as Phi Beta, on many campuses it has as high a standing, especially in the South and West. And it's my first honorary society so you can judge how thrilled I am. It remains for me to prove to the men that their confidence is not unfounded.

Saturday I figure that I'll need a bit of relaxation so I'm going to Scranton with the Glee Club. *What* a week! "Never let your studies interfere with your college education," is a maxim I have laid down.

To Girl Tuesday night.

You said not so long ago that nothing seemed to go wrong with me, that I was having no opposition, that all was apparently smooth sailing. Well, tonight was one instance to the contrary. How *wretchedly* I spoke in our trial debate! Oh, I was so disappointed and discouraged because I had had just two hours off in nearly twenty-four and Herb Brown expected me to give a finished case. But I'm just not built that way; I'm not clever; I have to plod along until I hit upon the solution—Oh! tonight I could cheerfully chuck the whole business. But that's where you come in, and where Mom and Dad, and all my friends come in. I can't back out, I must go ahead and give my best in spite of the fact that I'm not a debater, and I'm so glad that I have you all to *make* me do the thing I must do. There, I feel better and now I must sleep so that I can come back tomorrow. By heaven! I'll show 'em. Herb said "Nice work" to me tonight and then changed the subject quickly. By Friday night if I don't have an indestructible case—well, by George, I *will*, that's all. I'm sorry to bother you but I have to tell somebody.

Wednesday night.

Didn't I tell you I'd be feeling better? I spent all afternoon on the debate material, completely tossed aside my old speech and wrote a knockout second one. Tonight I gave it and Herb is smiling now. We'll win Friday night, or if we don't we will give the best possible case that has been presented on the negative side. I'm just itching for my chance; my nerve has come back for some unaccountable reason, and well, I'm just top-notch. Lead 'em to me!

Thursday night.

Hi, you! Say, I'm riding on the crest of a wave, but by George it's a wave I made myself. Tonight I showed Herb that I am not an imbecile and he said "Nice work" with some feeling. Truly, it was the best rebuttal that I've ever made and oh, but I'm happy!

You know, five years from now I'll look back and say: "Well for heaven's sake, did a little thing like a debate worry me?" To be strictly truthful I was not worried—I was scared stiff!

Dearest Family,

Hoist the flag; proclaim the good news, spread abroad the marvelous tidings; Larry helped win his second Intercollegiate Debate.

URSINUS—0
vs
LAFAYETTE—3 !!!

I came through tonight. Not as well as I can do, but thank heaven there's always room for improvement. You know old Percy Marks said a lot of nonsense, but here's one thing I like that he said: "If you continue to think, to work, to learn, to love—you may, by the Grace of God, become a Man!"

Only a month before I talk to you and tell you all about it, and by then I will have been in two more debates. I'm gone on them now, win or lose—because *I know that I have it in me to give my best!*

VICTORY

Theme for English

THE tree was the personification of victory. For years it had struggled with the blasting gales which swept the sheer and barren crags; snow and sleet had not killed it, nor rocks, nor droughts. With tortured and twisted trunk, its leafy arms were stretched toward heaven in eternal defiance of the inexorable elements and in mute supplication for life and strength.

I can visualize it now; it so perfectly embodied my emotions that the picture was indelibly engraved in my memory. Silhouetted against an autumn sunset, on the top of the world, it strained against the wind; strained, its broad breast exposed

Send the following message, subject to the terms on back hereof, which are hereby agreed to

February 23 1935

To Mr. Thomas J. Foster

Street and No. (or Telephone Number) 174 Prospect Street

Place Ridgewood, New Jersey.

Loads of happiness and success to the very finest dad that a fellow could have. My most used criterion for self-criticism is: "would this make me just a bit more worthy of my dad?" You see how you have permanently ruined me! But no matter how many things people say of me, good or bad, the thing that makes me swell most with pride is to be called:

"Tom Foster's Son."

SENDER'S ADDRESS FOR ANSWER

SENDER'S TELEPHONE NUMBER

and its muscled legs braced. It was old and bent and weather-beaten, but every line, every part of the tree joined in the one joyful symphony: victory!

To Girl

First of all I must get debating off my chest. I shall not bother you much more if I can help it, but do you realize what I suddenly woke up to yesterday? All my life I have dreamed of going to college; to me that seemed the acme of age and attainment—and after-life in business as a dim unreality. Here I am, taking an active part in college and looking forward to something more which is coming closer, and I am almost afraid of its proximity! But more than college itself I have looked forward to competition with other colleges, naturally in the field of athletics. And yet it suddenly occurred to me that I *am* representing Lafayette in intercollegiate circles—and that I am representing something *more* than the physical. Oh! *do* you see what I mean? Anyone else would see only the sour grapes in that I cannot play football or baseball, or that I am merely high-hat enough to rank as an "intellectual" because I am debating. But that isn't the point; it is that after all one is controlling other men; swaying them not by a twenty-pound superiority in weight, but by the even more telling effect of combined logic and personality! The possibilities are enormous and a bit terrifying—but of course they are just possibilities.

The 27th I'm going on a deputation for the week-end, and after that and the vacation I'll settle down like a good child in the last month of college to do a bit of work. For you can realize what my average output has been as far as scholastic work goes. Phi Bete? Huh, I'm liable to be kicked out or declassified! And then we have a strong hunch that several of us are going to start the old tradition of putting out a literary magazine. Bill and I are going to write a novel or series of essays or something, and I'm just going to spend as much time as possible in writing.

My summer is definitely settled. I am going to Arizona to a new boys' camp. It means the entire two months on ponies in the most beautiful part of the country—and only a few men have been there before. I lie awake dreaming of it.

PROSPECT

I'm dreaming of the forests, and the wilds of mountain ranges;
I'm waiting for the welcome day when I'll go back again;
I'm yearning for the wholesome air that sweeps the open spaces;
I'm pining for that old free life—beyond the world of men.

I'm tired of hasty living in this world of man's own making;
I'm weary of this headlong race with money as the goal.
My body's sick, my brain's tired, and my spirit is protesting—
I have a kindred feeling for the frightened, sightless mole.

So when I'm at the office, or stand sweating in the subway,
My thoughts persist in slipping to that summer—two years back—
I dream of mighty hemlocks nodding gravely at the heavens,
Throwing deep and cooling shadows on my rough-hewn timber shack.

For I cut the logs in winter when the sap was down the tree-trunks
And I let the lumber season 'til the warmer spring days came.
Then I built my little cabin by a dimpling, gurgling streamlet,
And I called it "Sinner's Heaven"—just to give the place a name.

I remember rising early from my bunk of fresh-cut balsam
Just before the sun came bursting through the orchid-tinted mist,
And I bared my head, and wondered at the silence of all nature
While the gray rocks blushed to crimson like a girl who's just been kissed.

The glory of the thin crags jutting boldly in the blueness!
How the legion ranks of massive clouds march grandly past the peaks!
Far below, before the spear-points of the firs melt into valleys
The walls stretch up to sheer cliffs where an eagle soars and shrieks.

The summer sky is angry and the gold-rimmed clouds have blackened;
Like the forked tongue of an adder spurts the lightning's searing flash,
While the drumming of the warm rain on the mountain's mighty bosom
Rolls a steady muffled beating to the thunder's splitting crash.

But thunder storms of summer are like passion storms of childhood,
And after rain and tear clouds glow the radiant smiles of calm.
So the sun goes blazing down behind the flaming west horizon
And the soft gray veil of twilight soothes the tired world with balm.

LARRY

The clouds are piled like whipped cream, and the cliffs are
splashed with scarlet;
The purpling haze has risen, left the valley deep and black;
And through the fresh-cleaned sky there gleams a blue-white
twinkling diamond.
The orange moon swings slowly up to start her silver track.

The magic of the moonlight and the mottled silver shadows!
The racy tang of hemlock in the fragrance-laden air!
Far away a fox is barking, and a hoot-owl's tender love song
Haunts the hills with plaintive sweetness, like a motif sad and
rare . . .

So I'd steal back to my cabin through the stately pine cathedrals
With my heart so full to bursting that I'd fight to keep it in;
And I'd watch my dying campfire; sit, and watch, and mutely
worship;
There was no one near to share it—and my solitude was sin.

* * * * * *

God never made such beauty for the pleasure of the eagles!
Nor planned that man should live apart. Oh! I believe in Fate.
So I left the teeming woodlands; I, of all this folk, was lonely;
My life was bare and incomplete—'til I could find a mate.

And I've found her! God ordained that from the millions I
should find Her.
Next April we'll be going back; our plans are all precise.
I'm dreaming of the glorious day we'll worship there together—
And my cabin "Sinner's Heaven" we'll rechristen "Paradise!"

To Girl

You don't mind if I try my new Corona? You see I have needed one for a very long time and it was only today that I had the nerve to actually put out the cash; it seems like such a lot to spend on a luxury—and yet I really do use the thing a great deal. And my other one was completely ruined by the other men in the House. This shall not undergo their treatment 'cause I have the key with me.

We went to Hopewell on a deputation team this last week-end. I am more firmly convinced than ever that we *get* far more than we can ever hope to *give*. And yet this time we put over a real piece of service to the community. We found that there was little or no harmony between the faculty and the students of the high school. In a discussion group yesterday afternoon we got the facts of the case, talked over all possible remedies, and then drew up a tentative resolution which the boys will submit to the school board and which will make, I am sure, for better understanding and coöperation. They will form a Student Council, get more good dances, and secure more intelligent eligibility rules. All these things when the boys in the school were just about ready to burn the place down—and now they are talking about how they can secure better results with the faculty. If that isn't an improvement then the trip was a failure.

I was with the most delightful family, but the father was a rabid fundamentalist, and whether you know what I am or not you know that I am not a fundamentalist, so last night when I had to get up in church I was scared to death that he might have come—and that I would have little chance to spend another night under his roof. But he didn't come, for which I was duly thankful. They were fine to me, and I hope that I may return sometime soon to help carry on the work that was started so well.

I have a confession to make: after the service last night I could almost have been persuaded to become a minister. It was the first time that I have ever spoken on such a subject before a large congregation, and I admit that the thrill was almost intoxicating! But I'd probably get the same thrill selling horse liniment.

I'm sorry that you think I would lecture you about your spree. I'm sure that I am not the one that has the right to pass on what you should do; and when I think carefully over the few people I know, I can find no one who *is* able to condemn. Quite the contrary. I think you should be congratulated on achieving *three* desires in *one* night!

And although you stayed in New York until X hours in the morning, which isn't quite au fait, why shucks, when you are old and wrinkled you'll blink your eyes—which will be just as bright and sparkly as ever—and tell your grandchildren of the fun you had and the thrill you got out of that evening in New York. That's the kind of thing you'll never forget, Girl, and something like that is necessary to all of us every once in a while. My trip to Bushkill Park last spring was like that—but I got a mump! Did you ever see the poem I wrote on that sad occasion?

A MUMP

With a sticky poultice against my cheek
  And a hot pad on my chest,
All wrapped up in a sky-blue shawl;
  (A color I detest!)

With an appetite like a hungry wolf—
  Over *calories* they debate—
On the dismal day when I caught this mump,
  I sadly ruminate.

Oh, then the days were merry and bright,
The world was all in song.
I laughed and sang with the rest of the gang
And gleefully romped along.

Now everything is dark and drear,
At least within these walls;
I sulk, and fret, and can't forget—
Inaction on me palls.

My attitude has changed, you see,
(My face has also changed).
And now that I can't go out at all
I fear I am deranged.

Here's my conclusion; this great old world
Is heaven when one is well;
But the same old world, with the aid of a mump,
Is sure to look like hell!

But to get back to you, if you were crazy about doing things like that all the time and went out of your way to pull some dumb trick—that would be different, and I should certainly spank—but no, I wouldn't. I wouldn't care that much. The very fact that you felt a bit squeamish about what you had done proves that it was loads of fun and a darn wholesome sort of stunt. Yes, I'm sorry, but I can find no reason for scolding—fact is, I let out one joyous shout when I read it, and I like you better.

Classes have been so much more interesting since I came

back. I'm just in top-notch trim anyway and feel like a *billion* dollars. And the days! Glory be, what weather! The trees are almost all out, just little delicate shoots and leaves—and much forsythia—and magnolia—and the wisteria is almost here. And the clouds are great billowy cotton things in the spring blue of the sky—you know. The earth smells different somehow, and the birds make an awful racket and chatter. It has all inspired me to the following small effort:

SPRING

A tinge of green, a flash of
        gold and blue,
A prinking robin's
        twittering,
A faint fresh fragrance
        from an earth
          that's new . . .
It's Spring.

I have decided to take it slow and easy. Not that I am slacking in my work; far from it. I am doing more than I have done before this year in class work. But somehow I'm not *rushing* the way I used to; just trying to do what I can and not worry about it, and the result is a very much more comfortable happiness. I am doing more with less waste time and energy; that is all. Maybe in two more years I will have learned to study.

Dearest Folks,

I was arguing with myself and hashing over this and that today until I got restless as a cat—just trying to decide on what my major shall be next year. I have decided—English

—which, as you know, cuts out Math and chemistry next year, substitutes the arts for them, and makes it extremely improbable that I'll ever go to Rensselaer. *Which* also cuts out engineering, at least any field work, *which* takes a load from my poor attempt at a mind.

You will say that now I should be entirely comfortable and decided on everything. I'm not, for just as this was all done and I saw visions of graduate work at Cornell in architecture with a year abroad in study, along came the chaplain and Dr. Ray Petty and quite upset my delightful frame of mind by challenging me (all unconsciously, of course) to the work they are in. I am quite serious when I say that for the first time in my life I considered the ministry—and I am still considering it. Write and tell me what *you* think and in the meantime I think I'll get into my slicker and walk off my restlessness in the rain.

RAIN

I like to feel the beat of the drops
The sting of the pelting rain,
The slippery suck of the yielding mud,
The swirl of the gaping drain.

I like to hear the roar of the storm,
The steady tattoo on the trees;
The swish and the lull of the swaying corn
Like the swish and lull of the seas.

I like to see the somber clouds,
The red of the muddy lane;
The soft gray veil on hills and fields
Of undulating grain.

LARRY

I like the smell of steaming earth,
The fragrance of dampened hay,
The acrid odor of rubber and cloth—
The freshness of the day.

While I stump along in my old high boots
And splash through puddles and streams,
My mind is busy with pleasant thoughts;
I dream most pleasant dreams.

I remember hours that have flown away
In a kind of golden haze;
I think of the times that are yet to be,
The joys of future days.

With none to share my lonely path
Except some huddled cows,
Who stare at me with dreamy eyes
And quite forget to browse.

I none the less enjoy the calm,
The solitude, the peace;
From toil and care, and other folks,
I feel a glad release.

Others may live in city walls
In cramped security;
But fields, and roads, and open skies—
It's here that I am free!

It's pleasant to hear the dripping eaves,
The plash on the window-pane;
But give me my poncho, boots and hat—
I want to be out in the rain!

Dearest Family

Was any child so fortunate in his "pay-rents" as I am? Truly, I was darn clever in picking out you two. The letters I got from both of you these last days were so fine and helpful and *good* that I can't tell you how much I loved 'em. Both are literature to me and I shall keep them always.

Naturally, as I said before, the idea of the ministry is so new and so different that I was more or less balled up on Sunday. All that I am doing now is officially considering it; before this I have immediately dismissed it. I still lean strongly toward architecture. Sunday night Mr. Detwiler—one of America's foremost artists, graduate of Lafayette and Zete—is to talk at Vespers on "Architecture in the Colleges." I shall be there and have a talk with him.

I have been elected to the Maroon Key Club—an organization to take care of visiting teams, etc.—hospitality committee, as it were. I was also appointed chairman of Social Work in the Y for next year. Our policy is to popularize the Y on the campus.

I am sitting in at a Lecture, but as far as anyone listening—why, it just isn't done. We have a great big Pennsylvania Dutchman for a Prof; he has the most porcine face and expression I've ever seen. Much wide face, shiny and pink; small blue eyes set closely together; and the loveliest colloquialisms you've ever heard. All the fellows around me are doing cross-word puzzles and reading magazines. Gee, it's a great class!

I had more darn fun last night. The combined musical

clubs went to Bath (rather a wet trip) and tried it out on the dog, as it were. We really put it across very well; Glee is snappy and peppy, and the Instrumental Club is perfect. The funny part of it was the auditorium. We held the concert in one of the churches, lacking a better place. We were jammed tight against the altar rail when we sang, and the orchestra —oh, it was really awful!—the drums were right between the two pulpits, the air from the saxophones made the altar-cloths flutter, the big brass horn was blatting right beneath a life-size painting of the Good Shepherd—and the clarinet was peeping coyly from behind the baptismal font! Holy smoke, you should have seen the people's faces; good old church-going, orthodox people! But what did they expect us to do in their church—sing hymns?

Anyway we had a lot of fun and I think that in spite of their religious prejudices they liked it too.

I went to Illy's for supper Friday night and their baby *is* getting adorable. I'm afraid Bob will spoil her, drat it all. He loves to pick Carol up and make her laugh and now the little thing yells when he puts her down. Friday she screamed and raved for ten minutes and scared them into sensible thought about her. It was a darn good thing.

I'm spending all of my time getting my composition and reading up to date.

Yesterday afternoon we liked the basketball game, 'cause we won it, and liked the tennis tournament in spite of the fact that we lost. I eat and sleep and play tennis and do Calculus—and keep right on being more crazy than ever about the two loveliest parents in the world!

To Girl

If I ever wanted to see you for just a second it was last night after the dance. I was waiting for Bill, who was taking a girl home. He would be back in fifteen minutes and then we would walk back to our House. Well, he had just left when the only man whom I dislike in the whole darn club came up to me and told me that he was stuck with two girls and wanted me to help him out—get them home—"only take a few minutes."

Well, I was suspicious and after the first half-hour was frankly skeptical. An hour later I was sorry I'd bitten. The man who got me in the jamb was having a mean party with his maid, and I, being out in the cold in more ways than one, had to play the fool and amuse my maid for all that time. After I had talked about everything from college to cheeses and back again, walked up and down the block a dozen times hoping she'd freeze or get pneumonia or something, she began to get really coy and chummy and insinuating, and damn it all, I near poked her one in the nose and beat it for Bill. Fact is, I was so sore and sick that I had to waste a night like that (most *heavenly* moon) on such a mud fence (which is slander for she wasn't bad looking) that I almost took her up just to get even with her. It never reacted on me that way before, but when she started this fool flirting and playing with my hands I was almost tempted to give in to myself and show her that that kind of stuff is not for wholesale fooling, and end up by spanking her soundly.

Well, I hope I played the gentleman; I'm sure I never

had to work so hard. The man finally showed up and after bickering around with the father of one of the girls for a long while (he didn't want his daughter to go out with strange men, yet he was lit to the gills on stuff from his own cellar!), they finally took us home and I wasn't sorry.

When I saw that tail light disappearing down the street I felt sort of weak and wanted you very badly, for it was a close shave for Larry.

Oh, well, the old moon grinned at me for a while and I felt better. Then I went in and Bill was waiting for me and the kidding he gave me snapped me out of it pretty quickly. The boy's a peach. I wish he wasn't a senior.

So I took an awful beating last night. That is, from the point that they think I'm an awful stick and antediluvian. Well, let 'em. As long as you typify my ideals I am quite ready to get myself in any jamb, 'cause I can pull out when I have something to hold to—and that something is the thought of you.

You asked me how you helped me. I can't say it very well, but this is something of what I'd like to say:

For over three years, Girl of Mine,
   I've known you pretty well;
How much you've come to mean to me
   You know I dare not tell.

I like your body, for it's strong
   And beautiful, and fine.
Your life is clean and wholesome, like
   I'm trying to make mine.

I like your mind; pure, eager, quick,
Your intellect is keen;
Your thoughts are fair, unbiassed, rich,
While mine are small and mean.

I like your spirit. You're a Heart,
A Personality.
Your sweetness and your lovely Self
Tell what I ought to be.

In body, mind, and spirit, Girl,
Your life is full and real;
Because I'd like mine that way too
I cherish your ideal.

And so you do all this for me
That no one else can do;
I pray to be more worthy, see?
More worthy, Girl, of you.

Forgive me, but I want you to have this that I scribbled off two weeks ago and hadn't the courage to tell you!

Yesterday was a big day. After lunch I fussed around until two-thirty and then took the Traill Green Math Prize exam. At the end of three hours I was only three-quarters of the way through and had to leave so there isn't a prayer of my getting even second in it, but it is good experience to have.[1] And *then*—! I hurried over to Wash Hall and arrived in time to go through the Tau Kappa Alpha initiation and now I am a Brother. It is such a good bunch of men! And after the ceremonies we had a regular business meeting and I was

[1] He won the prize.

elected vice-president for next year. More luck that I don't deserve. Then we went down to a dinner at the Karldon and Prexy and several other guests were there to make it real festive. Everybody said something and it was loads of fun all around—except that Herb will go next year and we were almost in tears when he made his speech.

So I've reached another goal that I have always wanted—and was sure I'd never get. Tau Kappa Alpha will increasingly mean a lot to me, and the next two years of debating will be one long joy. It would be deadly with the standard type of debaters—milk-and-water affairs with horn-rimmed glasses—but this aggregation is a fighting crowd and it is a pleasure to work with them.

Somehow all the little disturbing things are getting under my skin and my usual placid disposition is getting irritable. Will you let me rave if I promise to be irritable only to you?

The trouble started sometime this week with several fool little things that are the result of carelessness and irresponsibility. My relationship with J—— has never been terribly strong on account of them because no matter how hard we both try, we aggravate each other a bit, and it's a damn shame. I wouldn't care if I didn't like the boy so well, but when he goes out night after night and cares absolutely nothing about his work it makes me just *sick* for him. If he just would *say* that he doesn't care; but every week he is full of good intentions and he is a poor finisher. *Always* dies on first. Oh, I never say anything much, but when the man you would like for your friend is such a dismal failure, when two or three men in the House are accepting all the responsibility (how

Zeta Psi House, Lafayette College

"I liked the Zetes a lot:
I seemed to
fit in."

I've come to shy at that word!), when the House average is going for a merry ride downhill, when one has not a real friend to console with in the House—you must see that it is quite a job to keep a grin on your face and be nice to everybody. What they need is somebody who won't be nice, but after harping, harping futilely for nearly a year it's getting tiresome work alone. This sounds terribly bad for the Zete House, but truly the same and usually worse conditions exist in the other Houses.

The other afternoon after Senior Pee-rade Bob and J—— and I saw a peach of a show and just as I was about happy and contented I got in with a bunch of men and after driving around we ended up in Charlie's and I had to be sociable while the rest guzzled beer for an hour. Naturally that took the pep out of everything—for me, of course—and then I came back to the House and met Bro Perry from the Central Office.

He had come to talk to the men about scholarship and he dragged me aside (you must forgive me this telling but I want you to know) to tell me that one of the men in the House had said that—this sounds bad!—I was his ideal on the campus. Then after making me thoroughly uncomfortable Bro Perry wound up by telling me that I had a tremendous *responsibility* to the men, the House, and Zeta Psi, that I must watch myself every minute, etc. Damn! I went up to bed and was sore for a good hour, sore because I know well that it is true. I *have* a responsibility, and I'm trying to accept it, but it's hard sometimes. It's all right for other people to say, "Oh, so-and-so looks up to you. You must come clean for his sake." Sometimes I believe that this business of being an idealist isn't all it's cracked up to be; at least I'm sure that most times it's blamed lonesome.

Last night was the Theta Delt dance and after I had fully determined not to go I went, mainly for the fun of wearing my tuck. It was a great party; *marvelous* music, bunches of imported girls, and much life and gaiety. Guess that's what I've been needing; I've stayed too close to work and meetings.

Tuesday we went swimming in the river and it seemed mighty good to let the waters glide around me again. The current is dreadfully strong, but it was good sport and cooled us off admirably.

Thursday night I went to see Betty and instead of the dance—which was called off—we walked up toward Paxinosa and talked *and* talked. Without exception she's the only girl in this dratted town that I've met who can talk intelligently or seriously about things that count. Maybe she doesn't like to but she bluffs awfully well then. It is fun to get her comments on the men in College and compare them with the fellows' own estimates of themselves.

I've been reading Thomas Hardy's "Jude the Obscure." Lord, what a pessimist! And Meredith's "Richard Feverel." What a satire! But they are splendid books and I am still reading them with great relish.

We have a long report in English instead of a final exam, so today I shall start in on my criticism of Johnny Weaver.

SOPHOMORE YEAR

DUSK TO DAWN

Theme for English

FROM out of the west comes a tiny pin-point of fire. It pierces the dusk by its blaze; it is the harbinger of night in all her loveliness. Subtle changes take place; the deep shadows begin to soften, the trees whisper together, the grassy spaces become fairy playgrounds, a luminous radiance mantles the world. The harvest moon, peeping through the branches of the trees, gives a soft, warm light, changing Brainerd into a medieval castle, Pardee into a monument of living stone—and the Chapel into a place divine. Silhouetted against the sky, it personifies strength and beauty, truth and love; it reaches ever heavenward. High above shines Vega, perfect in her loveliness and purity, a burning diamond. She slowly circles above the Chapel as for centuries she has circled above other chapels; wayside crucifixes, Swiss monasteries, Greek temples, French cathedrals, Puritan meeting-houses—O inscrutable star, can you not be granted the power of speech to us this night?

"Men are trying to separate the sacred and the secular. *There is no distinction.* Man has a definite responsibility to his people and to his God. As the world must be bettered by his existence, he must regard his work as a sacred trust. Only when men live their religion seven days a week will they find true happiness."

The stars grow dim, the sharp contrasts fade, a bird chirps sleepily, and the growing rosy light in the East promises the dawn of a New Day.

PHILOSOPHY

I

SEVERAL times during the past year I have attempted to put on paper my philosophy—or, if that sounds too presumptuous for an eighteen-year-old, my ideas in regard to the most vital subject that has presented itself to youth from the beginning of time: what is the formula for life? Many will say that one must be at least fifty years beyond my age to even consider the question; some will laugh and declare me harmless; a few will realize that this is primarily a problem for the young people of the world to consider. At all events, I shall enjoy reading these incoherent and unsophisticated pages some day in the future, when I shall have had time to put the ideas into practice. I wonder if they will be fundamentally the same; if they are merely unripened opinions which will grow into substantial, tangible certainties, when time and experience have mellowed them?

My other attempts have failed; I was discouraged at the poor unity, coherence, grammar—endless things which are immaterial to what I really want to express. Now, however, crude and unscholarly as these sheets are, they embody to some extent my thoughts about this fascinating subject of living.

The last few years my ideal of an all-round man or woman has been that he or she should be strong mentally, physically, and spiritually. When I first joined the Boy Scouts, I was proud to pledge myself "on my honor to keep myself physically strong, mentally awake, and morally straight." The three divisions have always appealed to me; I have measured my friends and acquaintances by them. But while they are separate and distinct each from the other, I think that one's religion is the effect of their combined causes—that is, you can always tell a man's religion by the way he treats his body, his mind, and his soul. Show me the way a man dances, let me hear him talking at a stag party, let me play golf with him, take me through his place of business and bring his employees to me; tell me what he reads, and what he does with his idle hours, if he votes, if he gives himself to his community—and then I'll tell you what his religion is!

If he is a Christian in all of these things—and by Christian I mean that he applies Christ's principles to the best of his ability—he can go to church but once in many weeks and I will not be shocked. Nor do I belittle regular church attendance. It is a very stimulating and inspiring practice. But I know so many people who "religiously" go to church *and* prayer meeting, who roll their eyes piously when their comfortable pastor repeats to them the same old things that they have heard all their lives about the Brotherhood of Man and the Fatherhood of God, the Trinity, and the Redemptive Love of Salvation—and who are laws unto themselves the other six days in the week. Oh, they are thoroughly respectable! But how few people there are who believe in a seven-day religion. I agree with Glenn Frank in his emphatic statement that "there is no distinction between the sacred and the secular." Emerson said that a man's action was only the picture book of his creed. Surely a man's religion is the way he lives!

Some people, however, say, "Whose business is it how I live? I can do as I please." Which leads me to believe that the greatest need in the world today (with the exception of a spirit of love), especially in our own country, is Responsibility. I have always felt that my body, my mind, and my soul were given to me to use for the betterment of my associates, my community, my nation; that I am the trustee of a Personality, and that I must regard it as a sacred trust. How else can I explain my presence here? I must be useful, "else wherefore born?"

Nor do I go around with a long face and contemplate my chances to save some fallen brother; I have a heck of a good time trying to lead a normal, healthy, happy, vigorous life. It is all so simple! I cannot understand the spirit which prompts some people to withdraw into themselves, like the friars of antiquity, and watch the misdeeds and heresies of their contemporaries through a telescope, and pray for their souls. Only when a majority of sober men go to a college dance is the booze-toping crowd forced to capitulate; only when honest, high-minded men get into politics will the political bosses and puppets be forced out; only when sensible Christians get into the common run of things will the other crowd come to its senses. It's got to come about by *doing* the thing, by action, rather than by the drawing away of skirts and the praying for souls.

Responsibility in the largest sense means to me self-sacrifice; and yet, I believe that we must give ourselves to others if for no other reason than selfishness, paradoxical as that may seem. I belong to a fraternity. If a brother of mine comes in drunk and gives the house a bad reputation, I shall suffer with the rest. So I waylay him, sober him up, put him to bed, and tell myself that my responsibility to the fraternity compelled me to do it. Rot, in nine cases out of ten—but it works. Another example is prohibition. The churches of this country and the women of the country did a great deal to cut out the evil of the corner saloon, but they would have been helpless had not American Big Business realized that our revenues might be increased with prohibition. Selfishness—but it worked. The churches have not yet learned the psychology of the masses. They are teaching that war is naughty, immoral, useless; all of which is true, but the same old story. Should they spend half as much time and energy in campaigns showing the loss of money to the people through war, and the increased prosperity which would undoubtedly result from a warless world, they would realize more rapid results, I am sure. A grocer said to me the other day, "Hit a man in the pocketbook, and you hit him everywhere else." Selfish, sordid? Yes; but if it accomplishes the altruistic and the spiritual, should we complain? That is what I mean by our responsibilities to others being prompted by selfishness; "cast your bread on the waters" —and it will come back *cake!*

But this is selfishness in the higher sense. After all, it is very difficult to distinguish between sacrifice and selfishness when we are considering whole masses of people. When we come right down to it, we give to and do for others largely because of selfishness; for we are not happy otherwise. I do not mean to be cynical, I do not mean to discredit altruism, I do maintain that there are two kinds of selfish motives; one for personal gain, and the other for helpfulness. I have said that I believe in the latter, that it is a rare and beautiful thing to find a man or woman who is devoting his or her life to the task of making others happy. I cannot politely voice my sentiments about the former.

II

Tonight, several of us were having a good bull-session. One of the men said that a friend of his wanted a spacious mansion in the country where he could spend his days as a bachelor. He would read good books, have plenty of wholesome recreation with his hunters and his dogs, entertain a great deal among a congenial circle of friends, travel to new places a part of every year—in short, find happiness through seeing life in its most gracious and becoming aspects. I held that he would not find happiness; that he would become restless and discontented, and end up by wondering what he had proved by being alive at all. Because he would be living to himself. Happiness *is* the goal toward which we all work, the pot of gold at the end of the rainbow, the cherished ideal of our dreams—but how shall we find it? The Koran says: "Happiness must be earned." Christ said that we will find happiness only in proportion to the happiness that we give others.

So once again we find our definition of selfishness to be helpful. We desire happiness because we are human, we know that we cannot be happy until we give ourselves unreservedly to the task of making others happy, and so we do that—and find our pot of gold. This is selfishness, but in the higher sense.

Someone asked me why I came to college if it is not for selfishness. In trying to answer him I cleared up some points that I have been hazy about for some time. I came to college because I want to increase physically, mentally, and spiritually to such an extent that I can command a great deal of influence and win the confidence, the respect, and the love of other people. Pure selfishness. *But* I mean to use this influence in bringing happiness to these other people; through the medium of politics or architecture, or engineering, or the Y. M. C. A. I mean to do my utmost to make the Christian way of life the *only* way of life. Incidentally, if I can prove that the matter of being a Christian is not a mollycoddle idea, but a red-blooded, two-fisted, daring scrap from start to finish, I shall feel that I have accomplished a lot toward the ultimate goal.

Many people start out on the plan above—that of fitting themselves—but they lose the determination to carry on their work in the enjoyment of the conditions they have built up. For instance, a man may start out in his college career with the definite idea of climbing to a position from which he can command most, and for the greatest good. He reaches the position by hard work; he is president of the class, on the college paper, in several honorary societies, and outside activities. All the chance in the world for a marvelous influence—unlimited potentialities. Then, because of vanity or flattery, always something unworthy, he loses his ideal of sacrifice, his desire to be of aid, and he becomes impossible, a nonentity, a parasite. He reached third base, and died; he lost his opportunity. Suppose another man started out with the same idea and reached a similar position of influence. He controlled public opinion through his position, his pen, and his persuasiveness, for the highest ideals on the campus; he made a radical change for the better along some lines. He made a glorious dash for home—and won the game.

Now, both used selfishness (if you will) to gain position. In physics, potential energy is "energy of position," and must be stored up before it is expended as kinetic energy; the weight of a pile driver must be hauled to the top before it can be in a position to do work. In the same way, both of these boys got their potential energy; one of them didn't have his guide rods in place, and the force of his weight, unaimed, was spent on trivial and superficial things; the other sent all of his weight crashing squarely on the top of the pile—and his objective was driven home! The selfishness of the first man changed to self-advancement for self, and his selfishness became a sin; that of the other was self-improvement for others, and his selfishness became a virtue. Into these two branches is selfishness divided for me.

III

Convention is the real enemy of youth. Not the convention that prompts one to use the same fork that the hostess is manipulating with such charming ineffectuality, or that necessitates a black butterfly instead of a white bat tie; these are relatively unimportant, and have rather a wholesome effect than otherwise. But the convention of which we should be afraid is the insidious something that causes the endless whispering of the crowd: "Conform! Conform! Join us, and be like us!" Individuality is discouraged, personality is disparaged, ingenuity is criticized, novelty is frowned upon.

For because the trend of a cycle of society is reactionary, each unit of society plays its little part in retarding the march of the progressive. Such units as the family, the social set, the fraternity, the college, the business, the political party, or the church of a man exert their own particular pressures on him to make him conform—be one of them—share their views—preach their doctrines—hold their faiths and creeds—in short, the secret aim of each seems to be to turn out all of its members as nearly alike as possible. As these groups are, to a large degree, successful, the result is an overwhelming majority who have conformed, who are average, and who are thus mediocre.

The average is always mediocre, by definition. Psychology has given us the normal curve, holding true for large numbers of individuals, and the maximum height is always at the fifty-per-cent level, the average, tapering down to the subnormals on one side and the abnormals on the other. So we have this large middle group, this mediocre body, the criterion of dress, ethics, manners, intelligence, morals—at once the teacher and critic of the younger generation, who are taught that the acceptance of social pressures rather than the dodging of them, is the pathway to happiness and success.

Naturally, this control exercised by the majority is not the worst thing happening to the youth of today. A certain amount of convention is absolutely necessary, of course. Because of better living conditions, a higher standard of intelligence, and a code of ethics which is progressing all the time, this mediocre body is rising gradually to a new level, and their control is making for better and finer life—slowly, to be sure, but steadily. The common folk are on the upward trend. There is no question that the mediocre is leveling *up* the standards of the world, bettering conditions in all walks of life.

But as certain as it is leveling *up* the lower strata of society, it is leveling *down* the upper! It seems that the sands of progress are running into a huge glass, piling up to a peak, like a cone; but when the cone is nearly pointed, the sand slips down the sides, and while the average level is raised, the cone has lost its peak. The leveling up is a step in advance; it is in the leveling down that I am chiefly interested.

William McFee struck the keynote when he said: "In any sphere where all start at a prescribed age, as in great universities and public services, there is a tendency to become standardized, to be only one example of a prevalent type. Ambition is coördinated, jealousy is neutralized; and the hot lava flow of individualist passion cools and hardens to an admirable degree of solidity and composure. One's exact contemporaries are around in throngs." There's the evil: the tendency to become standardized, to be only one of a prevalent type.

We need to look no farther than our own college for examples. Within four months after their arrival, nearly all of our fraternity freshmen are wearing the same style of clothes as their fraternity brothers, the same tilt of the hat, the same size cuff on their trousers, the coat collar rolled the same way; one can almost recognize a man's fraternity by his dress. The pity of it is that this conformity doesn't stop with the physical appearance of the men; I merely pointed out that these conditions are commonplaces in the relatively unimportant side of college life; when we consider that in much the same way the mental, the social, the moral attitudes of the individual begin to be tainted by the attitudes of the group, the situation becomes far graver. Each subject alone requires a treatise, but it is fitting to touch a few of the salient points of each.

The majority of men come to college to learn; they are eager to study, to fit themselves for something, however far off in the haze of unmentioned dreams and aspirations that something may be. But a few months with men who have become somewhat hardened to these finer conceptions will, in most cases, cause a dimming of the ideal, a dropping of standard; the student will find that the prevalent idea of his associates is to get by with as little work as possible. There is little thought of meeting education half way. In many instances the desire to get something for nothing leads to the almost accepted practice of using outside aid in examinations. "Conform," the classroom whispers. "All of us are doing it and it won't hurt you just this once. What you do here will never make any difference to you later on in life. Conform!" —and there is the problem of cribbing.

An interesting problem in psychology is to sit with a group of men and hear the accepted social lion give his opinion on topics like dances and girls. Whether the men around him secretly agree with him or not, they all fall in with his opinion, making it the group opinion, and any contrary voice is promptly hooted down. Society begins early in life to play follow the leader, and the shame of it is that so many of the leaders are those who exercise an unwholesome influence. It is interesting also that the usual critic of a group is the man who sits around doing nothing, and who thus has more time to pass judgment on his associates than his busier mates, who are engaged in constructive work rather than destructive criticism. "Don't do that," he gibes the crowd. "That's a wet bunch to work with. Conform!"—and so we have our problem of extra-curricular activities.

Besides these problems of dress, intellectual laziness and negligence of social responsibilities—and more important—most of the troubles in morals and ethics arise from this conformance to social pressure. Here the leveling down is helped to such an unfair extent by the natural desires and frailties of human nature, that only the strongest of personalities, the most indomitable of wills, can successfully resist the opinion of the crowd. Ridicule is such a fearful weapon, and men find it so hard to face! "Come on," grins the crowd, "don't think that you're too good for us. Better men than you have done it; come with us tonight—conform, conform!" With fiendish persistence the mediocre exerts its tyrannical pressure—and there we have our most serious problems of intoxication and prostitution.

I have taken examples from college because they are most vital to us now, but the pressures of later life are as monstrous and as persistent. If a man joins a firm and finds himself in the midst of crooked dealings, he is not supposed to impart his knowledge; if an honest man tries to become a virile progressive politician—and a pathetic few are trying for that—he finds his way blocked by those who may lose money if conditions are improved. If a man wants to clean up a college campus, or put a finer type of play on the stage, or innovate fairer business methods, or preach his own interpretation of the truth, he has to buck the wall of conformity, the Great Mediocre, that sits back comfortably and complacently and sneers: "You can't do that while you're with us. We can't have our group open to criticism and ridicule; stay with us and conform, or away with you!" Not so much that they are defending dishonesty, but, as Randolf Bourne says, "It is simply the instinctive reaction of the herd against anything which savours of the unusual. It is the tendency of every social group to resist change."

Apparently few are willing to resist social pressure to expose themselves to the scoring that is sure to follow a definite stand for the individualist theory. Yet when we look to men who have been and are great, we find that in every case they have determined what they wanted to do, have had the courage of their convictions, and then have proceeded to the task, snapping their fingers at conformity and convention. Lincoln did it when he pledged himself to the defense of the Union; Roosevelt did it in his Civil Service Reform program; Wilson did it when half the world was laughing at him. Harry Emerson Fosdick is still preaching and he draws the largest congregations; Fred Stone is still putting on clean plays and he is getting the largest audiences. These men and others are giving the *truth as it is in them*, and the Great Mediocre, whether it approves or not, is forced to acknowledge its respect!

But it is of no use to criticize existing conditions unless a remedy is suggested, for to break away from the old pressures without a definite objective is obviously as radical and detrimental as accepting them blindly or willingly. So I want to make my plea a plea for personality and individuality. I am not advocating the overthrow of responsibility, but the realization of a greater responsibility to one's self, one's contemporaries, and one's nation.

First, a man must have his eyes open to the pressures exerted on him. If he conforms to the prevailing mode of dress, he must realize that he *is* conforming, and that all those who do not are probably as intelligent as himself. He must watch himself to see that he is not being forced into accepting the standards of thought and action of those about him. If he plays the violin, for instance, and dreams of the concert stage, it is entirely permissible for him to make money playing jazz *if* he realizes that he is conforming for the time being in order to further his future training. If he has to stop college because of financial difficulties, it is perfectly proper that he should work at any job to make money *only* if he sees clearly that he is conforming temporarily so that he can later finish his college education. He must not compromise his conscience.

And as he must see the present clearly, so must he see the future; he must have vision. He must put first things first; see life in its true perspective; have no delusions as to the relative values of things. And if he has a vision, let him keep it sacred and well guarded; if he wants to be a musician or a bricklayer, a painter or a minister, an architect or an ornithologist —in God's name, let him carry on in spite of criticism and ridicule, fitting himself for the task; dreaming, planning, working—dodging the pressures of society.

Let him leave them to their conformities and their conventions; they are impotent and permanently harmless. Let him ignore their scoffing, laugh at their jesting, and set his

"I'll call him 'Spunk,' " said Larry.
"He sure has it."

face toward the problem ahead, keeping his body and mind and soul clean for the conflict. Let him develop into a great personality; for if he continues to work, to think, to love, he may, by the grace of God, become a Man. Banish conformity! Substitute the Supremacy of the Individual for the Tyranny of the Mediocre!

ARIZONA

ANTICIPATION

(*Written on the train going to Arizona*)

Te-click, te-clack, te-click, te-clack, te-click,
Te-clack; the wheels ring out their strident song
That help to make this harmony of noise—
This symphony of discords. To the ear
The sound is not unpleasant—but a hum
Which was, and is, and is to be for hours.
The muffled rumbling of the heavy trucks
Is like the blending of the drum and tympany;
Each jolt and jar, the double bass; each scrape,
The brass; each piercing squeak, the violin.
The chorus sinks to dimness on the fields
And swells to a crescendo in a cut
Or tunnel; groaning like a thing in pain
When slackening speed to take a bridge or curve.
The clacking, clacking, dins into the brain;
Leaves no distinct impression of each noise,
But fuses all into one sense of sound—
A clacking, rumbling, harsh monotony.

The glistening rails go racing out behind
The observation platform; drawing near
Each other slowly, 'til they meet miles back
In steel embrace, just where the thick-piled clouds
Float down to pat the never-ending sand—
Like cotton batting on a sun-burned skin.

ARIZONA

All wires and poles and posts streak by the train
And slowly reach back to that single point
Until it seems that all are fastened there,
And that the train, unhooked, is slipping down
And off the world.

And all is hot and dry;

The body slips into a lethargy,
The senses dull with the monotony,
The mind leaps in to fill the vacancy. . . .
The rumbling echoes louder in my ears;
The thund'ring of uncounted hoofs
That hurl uncounted cows in wild stampede.
The air is pierced with frantic bellowing.
Across the range, the whirling dust-cloud rolls,
A screen for maddened cattle. In the din
The sharp stacatto cracks of forty-fives
Attest the presence of the cowboys. Now
The milling starts; outlined against a hill
The swirling mass is like an emptying bowl,
A lead-gray whirlpool, full of countless mice
Revolving toward the vortex.

But the scene

Has faded, shifted, brightened—'til I see
A pack train winding up a wooded ridge.
The air is sweet and cool. A gentle puff
Stirs towering red-trunked western yellow pines
To tender whispering. The twilight calm
Is broken by the stamp of hoof on stone,
The rattle of a pebble, tinkling chains,
And squeaking sweat-stained leather. . . .

And again

The picture changes. Through the richly deep
And velvet blackness of an autumn night
There flames a ruddy glow, and near the fire
Are half a dozen riders of the range
Enjoying taciturn companionship.

LARRY

A hemlock knot explodes; the fresh sap runs
And sizzles with a friendly spluttering.
Above the net of needled lace, the stars
Burn fiercely, brightly, from a million worlds,
And throw a softly glowing radiance
Upon the hills.

Kaleidoscopic views
These scenes may be, and yet they show so clear
So perfectly distinct in all detail,
They seem reality; a snow-clad peak
Splashed scarlet by a bloody sun; a range
Of undulating ridges stretching far
Into a haze of opal-tinted mist;
A yellow, barren, feverish desert floor;
The pungent smell of shrinking, burning flesh
As calves are branded; yelling, cheering men
At rodeo and round-up, where from all the
Countryside folks gather for the tests
Of strength and skill; a barbecue and dance;
A sun-baked village of adobe huts
All overrun with half-starved, yelping curs,
Fat, red-skinned babies, dirty, howling kids,
And black-haired frowzy women. . . .

Suddenly
A blue-white flash of lightning streaks
The steely sky, and forms a hissing spark
Between the low-hung massive thunder heads
And level miles of rock-ribbed mesa land.
A thick gray veil descends and blots out all,
And low menacing thunder warns a storm.
A closer flame, a splitting shock—again!—
Until the air is quivering like a nerve
Laid open with a knife. My ears feel thick
With such reverberation. Louder yet
And more insistent—rumbling, rumbling—now
A clacking, clacking, clack, te-click, te-clack

And I am conscious of the trucks again,
The swaying car, the torpid day, and that
The scenes have been inventions of my mind,
The creatures of imagination's play.

June, 1925

Monday, the 15th:

Dad and I drove into New York and he left me at the Grand Central. I sure wanted him to come with me, but maybe some day we can have a vacation together. Mother seemed pretty sorry to have me go, too. Wish I had a flock of brothers and sisters!

It was a nice day. The country was familiar so I read "Jane Eyre" and had a chance to get acquainted with "The Man in Lower Nine." His name was Mr. Beman and he is General Counsel for the Chicago, Rock Island and Pacific Railroad. He talked very interestingly of politics, history, psychology, literature—almost everything from science to sandwiches. He was a short, rotund, jolly man. The day was stifling, and we ran into several thunder and lightning storms which cooled off the car sufficiently to make comfortable sleeping. I missed the diner and ate imported Swiss cheese that was sweating fragrantly in Mr. Beman's suitcase. The night was fine.

Tuesday, the 16th:

We arrived at Chicago at 7:20 *some* kind of time; my watch stopped in despair after the third or fourth change. Of course, you can leave it at any time, and it'll be correct somewhere.

I had expected to go to the Santa Fe station to see about my reservation, but Mr. Beman took me to some friends of his—everybody knew him—in the Consolidated Ticket Offices only a block from the station, and all was fixed in a jiffy. Then he put me on the elevated for Oak Park to see Aunt Ida and left with my sincere blessing.

Wednesday, the 17th:

I left Aunt Ida and went to the Dearborn Station for the Santa Fe train. I finished "Jane Eyre," which is a darn good yarn, and then tried the observation platform. There were two or three folks who looked as if they might loosen up but nothing happened until a girl named Thelma Foster got on the train. She was sure a good sport. I wonder if she is any relation to me? Her folks are all in California. So we talked a while and then I went to sleep outside. When I woke, the platform was deserted and I had to lock up the train for the night.

Thursday, the 18th:

Things started off auspiciously by a jovial greeting from most of the car and a knockout breakfast at the Fred Harvey dining room. After a morning playing cards with Thelma Foster and Ruth Jones, and another good meal a la Fred Harvey, I wrote and finished "Anticipation," a bit of verse. Then came the mountains, and I took my banjo to the observation platform. The bunch unlimbered, and in ten minutes a whole crowd filled the last car. We sang for over an hour and only adjourned for dinner and until after eight. Then came two more hours of playing and singing with my good old banjo the center of interest. Gosh, it was fun! After a "good night" all around, I went to bed.

Friday, the 19th:

I got up early and decamped at Holbrook to the cheers of the gang that rose to see me off, bless 'em. Mr. and Mrs. Miles met me in their flivver and it was fine to see them again. They wanted to hear all about Ridgewood, of course, and I did my best for quite a while.

After lunch five of us, with Mrs. Miles, went to the Petrified Forest, and that was marvelous and quite awe-inspiring. It has only been there some millions of years.

Just before supper I met Fred Turley and right away I was very much impressed; he seemed an unusually fine man. Then the two girls, Jerry, a Mr. Stiner, and myself, went to a real Western dance, and I had the time of my life. Gee, it was funny, but there was good music and Ruth dances very well. I was *tired* that night.

Saturday, the 20th:

I left Holbrook with Fred and Leo, the latter a real bow-legged, hard, Texas cowpuncher. He is a scream, and I like him a lot now that I know him well. Fred had to stop once or twice on the way because he is postman for the district. We got to Airipine just before noon and I met Mrs. Turley. She is a dear and has two adorable kids, Stanley and Grant.

Soon after lunch sixteen of us started off in four cars and began a trip too glorious to give in full, but the bare outline is something like the following:

We arrived at Jacob's Well in a penetrating rain that

didn't make a wet party of it at all. I began to learn how to start a wet camp and convert it into a dry one. Then we ate and sang and went to our beds. I slept with old Leo and he pushed me into the rain, but aside from that it was a good night.

Sunday, the 21st:

I woke early because I was uncomfortable. After a good breakfast of meat and biscuit, we broke camp and, leaving our stuff there at Jacob's Well, went into Willow Creek Canyon. On the way we saw the Tonto Basin from the Rim and it was as great a sight as the Grand Canyon. It turned out a nice day, and after a cold lunch we had Indian wrestling and running and jumping. I ruined myself at the latter and was stiff two days. Then we ran back to Jacob's Well, got our stuff, and drove back to a bluff near Shovellin Canyon. We went down into the canyon to fish and went to bunks early.

Monday, the 22nd:

We left for the canyon early in the morning and fished all the forenoon. We had a cold swim, too. Fish for lunch was great, and then we caught loads more with our *hands!* Late in the afternoon we started back, and those blessed kids paddled all the way home as nice as could be. It was a hot, stiff climb.

We moved to just above Wilmer's ranch and made a quick camp for the night. I watched the stars which were out for the first time since I came. The days as well as the nights are cool in this part of Arizona, especially in the shade.

Tuesday, the 23rd:

The Flakes had left, so the rest of us rose early to get home. I drove the flivver over that mountain road and breathed more easily when I got back to Airipine. It was a glorious day with great clouds, and I was as lazy as I have ever been in my life. I wrote a hurried letter to Mother and to Girl so that Fred could take 'em to Holbrook when he left.

After a good lunch I got out a Kipling book and read for a while but got so sleepy that I had to stop. Met Jo Flake and Barr Turley. These chaps around here are sure fine and honest and hospitable. I went with Mr. Lewis and we saw them milk, and feed a little lamb, and I rode a yearling calf, to the discomfort of my legs; but it was fun. We ate again without Fred, and I fixed up my bunk for the summer. I have a dandy little cabin near the bungalow that I can claim for my very own. We all went to bed early.

Wednesday, the 24th:

And we all get up early! I spent a few hours roping and came within twenty feet of an object instead of in the opposite direction. But I guess I *can* learn. Then I spent the rest of the time reading and getting this diary up to date. Fred came by lunch time and brought a few letters.

I fussed around a while and then helped the men who are cementing the schoolhouse. Then I got Stockings, who is to be my pony, and had a dandy ride on him. Supper sure tasted good and I spent the evening with Fred and "Uncle Hi" Turley. I hobbled a horse for the first time and learned a bit of dry farming. Bed early.

LARRY

Thursday, the 25th: (From a letter)

I have just returned from a long ride, my second one, and I am a darn sight more comfortable in a rocking-chair than in a saddle. But yesterday Barr (Fred's brother) caught Stockings, their best cow pony, and I rode out for a while. The sunsets are magnificent, "Sundown Ranch," you know, and so late afternoon is just the time to go. But the summer rains are beginning and that means that I shall have to ride in the mornings.

This morning I started out on Stockings with boots, spurs, chaps, rope, hat, and everything—and of course felt funny as the deuce. I tried to look natural but it just wouldn't be.

So I left the ranch and struck west for a valley where Fred knew that the "Flying V" outfit was driving about 600 head of cattle to Holbrook. I rode from nine until 2:30 steadily and found the valley and one of the riders chasing stray steers, but he didn't know whether the outfit was behind or ahead. I helped him for an hour and we scared up two more steers and then came to some cedars, little squatty fellows up to 20 feet tall, and level country. Well, I lost the rider. I worried two steers around in the cedars, trying to hold them until I could find him, but he had vanished. Then I was high and dry. Every direction looked the same, and the sun was *exactly* over my head, so I kept the east breeze on my left cheek to keep myself traveling south. Of course I had a compass, but I want to get used to directions.

I was sorry I missed the drive because it must be fascinating to see so many head moving at once, and I wanted to see and eat at a real chuck wagon. But I got back at 7:30 and Mrs. Turley had a knockout supper waiting for me, so I didn't care.

Friday, the 26th:

Practiced roping for several hours. Fred went to Holbrook of course, and he expects to bring a boy back with him. I started polishing a steer's horn and went for a ride on Major in the afternoon because someone left the gate open and Stockings ran back to his pasture.

We played and sang in the evening, and I had a dandy long talk with Wilma (Mrs. Turley). She told me much about Mormonism, and I am convinced that it is a very wonderful religion. Still, I can see no more difference between a good Latter-day Saint and a good Methodist than between a good Methodist and a good Baptist. That is, as far as actual living goes.

Saturday, the 27th:

Worked on the horn polishing all morning. Have a dandy pair now. Fred came back bringing Bill Irving, a boy from Chicago, with him. Later in the afternoon Bill was fixed up with Major, and I rode on a new pony that just came in to water, King. He is sure a wonderful horse. Another magnificent sunset. We rode along the big pasture and saw no end of jacks and one coyote. I never want to leave this kind of life altogether.

LARRY

Sunday, the 28th:

The Mileses came in the morning, all except Mildred. They stayed all day. After a knockout dinner we fussed around and then Ruth, Chan, and I rode Major, Dick, and King over toward the Ranger Station.

After they went I had a real ride all by myself and the beauty of everything just sort of hurt me. We went to bed early to "prepare for the morrow."

Monday, the 29th:

We were all up early and anxious to be off. We started on our Grand Canyon-Prescott trip at just seven. At Holbrook I mailed the letters that I wrote the night before and sent a day letter to Girl so that she would get it when she arrived at camp.

We ate lunch at Winslow and kept on. The road to Flagstaff was awful. We stopped at Meteor Mountain and saw that heck of a hole right in the middle of the desert. We ran into thunder storms all afternoon and finally turned off on the Canyon trail. It was dark when we arrived, but we had covered some two hundred and thirty miles in that little flivver over terrible roads since seven A. M. We were averaging about thirty miles on a gallon for the week's trip. Imagine, we made the Grand Canyon in one day (sounds like Genesis!).

Camping that night was as much fun as ever. We saw the "Ditch" by moonlight, and I thrilled at it again. It rained in the night, but we didn't care.

ARIZONA

A MERE BAGATELLE

(A theme for class in English written about Larry's trip down the Canyon in 1916)

SLIP, slop, slip, slop. The gray burro's tiny hoofs beat a steady tattoo on the snow. I swayed drunkenly from side to side on the creaking leather and watched the ears of the little fellow flop up and down, up and down, in perfect rhythm. Every day for twenty years this sturdy beast had carried awed tender-feet down and up this marvelous fissure in the earth, this Grand Canyon. A very narrow ridge of bone and muscle separated me from a precipitous and hasty view of the Canyon's glories with little chance for enjoyment or reflection. I tightened my legs around his chubby sides, and permitted myself a more careful contemplation of my surroundings.

My trusty mount had reached a turn in the snaky trail and was slowly pivoting, all four feet bunched together—ridiculously inadequate for balancing, I thought. I leaned over his withers, and saw space; I glanced back over his rump, and saw space! A slight move would surely send us crashing into the hazy blue mists a mile below. There was a sudden lurch; somebody screamed; I grabbed the pommel and imagined myself falling into those waiting depths, dead, plucked at by vultures. . . . But I was being jolted down the trail again!

"Just a slip," grinned the guide.

My God!

LARRY

Tuesday, the 30th:

We left the Canyon early after we had been properly awe-stricken by the sunrise over the rim. Then we headed south. I had several good talks with Fred on the way, and we arrived at the Bates' Ranch outside of Prescott in the middle of the first real storm of the season. Mrs. Bates is Fred's sister, and we had no end of fun with that family all the time we were there. We hit the hay after celebrating Mrs. Bates' birthday with neighbors, music (on a real piano), and ice cream.

Wednesday, the 1st of July:

Bill, Ted Bates, and I walked up to Jupiter's Temple and stayed there all morning. The view from there was lovely and I had a gorgeous sun bath. Then we packed into the flivver and started on the seven-mile run to Prescott and the celebration.

I can't say very much about the Frontier Day Jubilee; it was so new and exciting and different. I saw calf-tying and steer-roping, bull and bronc riding that I had only dreamed and read of before. It was splendid—the whole business. Fred and I tried to sleep on the ground, but the mosquitoes drove us back to the porch. Moon's great!

Thursday, the 2nd:

We tried shooting my new six-shooter for a while; then tried calf-tying, Fred saved the calves by taking us swimming to Granite Dells. It was pure bliss to get in the water again. We went from there to the second day of the celebration, and it was the same, only more so.

We stayed in that town for a while, had supper, bought

some things, and went to the movies. More rain and lots of it. Then to the Bates' for the night.

Friday, the 3rd:

We left the Bates' and Prescott for home. We had seen about all there was to see, and Sundown Ranch looked good to us. We rode over the mountains to Jerome and Clarkdale, and I saw a typical mining town, and one of the big copper smelters. More rain. Who said that this was hot and torrid country? It cleared at lunch time, and we turned west to Montezuma's Well. The man who owns it and lives there is Mr. Back, and he showed us all around. There are cliff dwellings and caves and we explored a while. Then we left the main roads and turned to the mountains again.

We camped in a tremendous yellow pine grove just in time to see a glorious sunset that turned all the trunks to a dripping orange. Then the moon came up, and I was gone. Fred and I sat near the coals and talked late—until nearly ten—but Bill had gone to his tarp a while before, not feeling well. That is the way to sleep, out under the sky and fringed in by fragrant pine needles.

Saturday, the 4th:

Hoo-ray for George Washington! It was raining when we woke, but Fred made biscuits again. It cleared in a few hours, and I rode through the most beautiful country that I have ever seen, the Coconiño and Sitgreaves forests. It is impossible to describe their beauty; the first is all jungle undergrowth between the pines and firs; the second is like a magnificent parkway.

We ate lunch by the grave of some poor outlaw, and Fred kept Bill and me on pins and needles all the way home with tales of the younger west. We stopped at Promontory again and saw Calkins, and the rest of the way home was familiar to me, the same road that we covered two weeks before. We got home all set to surprise Wilma, but she had expected us three days later, and was visiting at Snowflake! But we had bachelor's supper, and I went to my li'l nest. It was another of those glorious nights; and better that I sleep than that I walk around and wish I were not alone.

Sunday, the 5th:

We expected Wilma before Sunday School, but she didn't come all day. I fooled around and read and wrote while Fred was at church, and we had more bachelor's meals. Poor Bill is starving 'cause we are eating Mex frijoles (beans, of course). In the afternoon I got Major and started for Lincoln Ranger Station. The air was glorious, and I cut across country. It is nearly ten miles. I met Perry Pierce there and talked with him awhile, and then started to bring two horses home with me. I found 'em all right, but they were in with about eight of Perry's horses. I cut them out after a time and started driving them home. Of the trials of the first hour I shall be dumb—probably was "dumb." They wanted to stay and everything was pulling for them, but I got them home. Later Lawrence Flake rode the little sorrel colt out after the cows and the latter stumbled, killing itself, and giving Lawrence a bad fall.

There was a full moon and Fred and I sat out in the garden and didn't say much.

We had covered some two hundred and thirty miles in that little flivver over terrible roads since seven A. M.

Fred, Bill and I rode three horses and took two pack horses—just to give us the experience with them.

Monday, the 6th:

I practiced roping all morning. It sure is getting better. After lunch I polished my cow's horns again and read Richard Harding Davis. Barr came in on Bird, driving King, so we have two more good saddle horses. Wilma came late in the afternoon with Mr. Lewis and Reg and "Aunt Roberta" Clayton. We had a nice visit, and after some songs with the banjo, etc., I said goodby and goodnight.

Dearest Family,

Well, we are home again from our Prescott trip and glad to be here. Not that we didn't have a great time, for we did, but it is mighty nice to fool around this here Sundown Ranch. I have never said much about the climate and the country, have I? Well, here goes.

Airipine (three houses and a combined post office and store) is a little higher than 6500 feet altitude. It is about six degrees cooler than Ridgewood all the time; the sun is hot, of course, but in the shade there is always a breeze and it is nice and cool. Every night I sleep with three blankets over me, and I need 'em all. I have worn a sweater at some time during the day every day that I have been here.

We are up past the line of scrub cedar and piñon; on the slopes all around are the large cedar and juniper, and the big western yellow pines start at the ranch. Only four miles south of us they start in in earnest and stretch for unbroken miles as beautiful forest—the Sitgreaves. The water is sweet and ice cold; we have green things every meal, and lettuce is one of the main articles on camping trips. In short, there is nothing disagreeable here; no snakes, lizards, or poisonous bugs, no mosquitoes, only flies of course, on a ranch, and they are not in the house. I am really serious when I say that I would give anything to find an occupation that would permit my living here in this district.

I'm gaining weight and strength rapidly, and I'm filling out. Fred is showing me how to box and is getting a punching bag. And oh! glory be! I wish that the summer would never end, that you would come here, and that we would live here forever! Gosh, I love you all!

Tuesday, the 7th:

Fred went to Holbrook again. Bill and I went with Barr to hunt some mares that had gotten out of the pasture. It was a great day; lots of clouds and fairly warm. We separated, and I ran on to a bunch of horses almost at once. They were driving well when Bill, not seeing me, came racing into the group and we lost all but three. As it happened, there was only one worth looking for in the bunch, a great brown maverick. He was immense, and wild as an Indian. Barr, coming up the draw, saw him and ran him for three miles, but it is killing on a good horse to chase a crazy one like that. If I were to be here long, I would sure get me a bronc, gentle him and train him myself.

Barr and I left Bill to watch the three horses, and made out to see if we could find any more. I met him again, both of us going to a sheep camp for information. They invited us for lunch and of course we couldn't refuse. Poor Bill was left hungry, though. But it was interesting to me to see the cleanliness of that camp. It was large—five men in all—with at least a dozen pack burros and nearly four thousand sheep.

They cooked in Dutch ovens, of course, and as usual the diet was frijoles and biscuits with syrup. Nice brown flaky biscuits! And there was fried potato with mutton, tea made from some plant, goat's milk, new to me and delicious, and boiled rice with raisins. What a feed! And everything spick and span. Those Spaniards were sure nice to us.

We came home with no mares and will have to try it again. We had an early supper and then I had to practice shooting and roping again. Three weeks ago if anyone had told me that in this short time I could handle a gun, rope calves, and ride twenty-five miles easy—well, I would have sure laughed at him!

My Dearest Family,

I loved Mother's last two letters. Especially the stories of the squirrel and Mrs. Tanager. I am getting acquainted with new kinds of bird and animal life; jack rabbits and loads of cotton-tails, and prairie dogs and coyotes, although the latter are mighty scarce and *mighty* fast. But the hoot-owls are thrilling at night. One sits in the tree near me and goes "poo, poo, poo, po ooo!" It has the sweetest, saddest song of all the birds. Then the mourning dove has a dismal little cry, and the night hawks have a piercing "peep." I was on a hill near us the other night and all of a sudden there was a rush of wings and a wild "peep" in my ear and I nearly fell over. I had come too close to a night hawk's nest. Sure enough, I found the little spotted eggs right on the ground with not even a twig for a nest.

It has been fun this week. Tuesday and Wednesday Barr, Bill, and I went to look for cows and horses that had got out of the pasture. You know it is so funny out here. A man will lose his finest horses and not mind at all. "Oh, someone will let me know where they are!" And sure enough, in a few days or weeks the message will come in by word of mouth through maybe twenty people that So-and-So's horses are forty miles away. And So-and-So just ambles down and gets them—if he can.

Wednesday, the 8th:

Barr, Bill, and I left early in the morning again to search for cows and "broomies"—horses running wild. We rounded up a bunch of long-horns and drove them down to the double tanks, seven miles north of the ranch. Then Barr and I went off and separated; we covered a lot of territory, and both of us landed on five of our cows and a bull. I drove them back to the tanks while Barr went on.

We met again, and Barr and I changed horses—he getting the best of it, of course, with King. Bill and I drove our cows home, and I nearly went wild because Dick, my gallant mount, couldn't even walk. By the time we reached the ranch, I was all in, but some letters cheered me up considerably.

After supper we went over to the Owen's and I had a lot of fun playing the piano. Gosh, it was great again. I went to bed early—and in the rain.

Thursday, the 9th:

I woke feeling lazy and stayed that way all day. I read a lot of Richard Harding Davis, and whittled cow's heads and shined cow's horns. We didn't ride, but I got enough exercise punching the bag that Fred put up, and put on the gloves with him. Otherwise I read and ate and loafed and had a glorious time.

Friday, the 10th:

I was all excited because I was going to Holbrook and that meant a hair cut and a bath! We took my boots and a saddle and left them at Marsh's in case he should find Midnight, one of Fred's best horses.

The Mileses seemed glad to see me again. After supper I took the bunch to the movies, and as it was the first one I'd seen for a month, I sure enjoyed it. We talked for a long while afterward; Stiner was there again, and the day was a success.

Saturday, the 11th:

Fred and I left Holbrook for the Flake ranch. Marsh and Jean and Bruce and I went after Midnight and got him, and then we rounded up some of the Flake cows. It is mighty warm in the valley. I was tremendously interested in the "sinks"—large holes in the ground that have just sunk and left great pitfalls. When we rode along we could hear the hollowness of the ground sometimes as if we were going over a bridge.

Jean and Bruce were breaking broncs, and it was fun to watch them, but I had a long ride in front of me so I left. My direction was "southwest," and I held to it for hours and hours it seemed. And I got so thirsty that I wanted to yell. I was lost, and the sensation was distinctly thrilling; but I kept on going, over hills and mountains and draws and ridges again, until I bumped right into the Government Tanks! Just the place I was going. Glory be, I was sure relieved. So I sipped the nasty water and came along the seven miles home. Tired? I was nearly dead.

Sunday, the 12th:

I went to Sunday School and believe me, whether the Mormons have the right dope or not, it is the most plausible and sane and scientific and *universal* that I've heard. And everyone from the littlest kid to the oldest man knows his stuff. There is no mystery, no wondering if there is something that had better be left unexplained; everything is clear and implicitly *believed* and *lived!*

The Mileses arrived for a visit; Ruth, Mildred, Stiner, and I went up toward Lincoln in the pines and had a real New Jersey picnic—*thin* slices of bread. It was a glorious day and I wished very hard for some of the kids that I know at home. Oh, I might as well be truthful—*one* of the kids. The nights are too beautiful.

To Girl:

At seven-thirty this morning Bill, Barr, and I went out again to get some horses. This has been the day of all days for me. I have been working with real cowboys and treated as if I were one of them. I worked thirteen hours with only a few minutes out for lunch, and that was about the only time I left the saddle. I drank water that had pollywogs in it, and ate stale beans, and they tasted good. And I handled the day herd, and helped drive the seventy-five head of horses all day, and most glorious of all, I chased wild horses and got 'em!

Glory be, I wish I could tell you, but as I must leave early again tomorrow I must sleep now.

Tuesday, the 14th:

We left this time for Double Tanks after we had branded some horses. It sure is hot, dusty work, racing the remuda [1] around and around! We drove the day herd down to the Tanks, and then the other men circled and put new horses in the round-up. It was another long day and everyone was really tired, but we brought the herd back to the corral for further treatment.

Wednesday, the 15th:

Branded some more and tied up several mules and horses to be broken. I am to gentle the little J-arrow horse, and I'll call him Spunk. He sure has it.

I read and wrote a bit after lunch. About five I went over to the corral again and started the gentling process of Spunk. I broke him to lead at first. Then we tied up a hind foot and I got him used to the blanket and saddle. And *then* I got on my first bronc! But as Fred predicted, he was in a sulk and wouldn't buck, and I sure took him for a good lesson. It was fun—like playing with dynamite; but he'll be a good horse.

Thursday, the 16th:

The Pleasant Valley Missionaries came and are two darn nice fellows from near Salt Lake City. The five of us, with Barr, spent the entire morning shingling the roof of the

[1] The herd of saddle horses used at round-up time is called a *remuda*.

cabins. Of course, that made us lazy for the afternoon. I read and wrote some letters, and finally went out to get my bronc. I mauled him and "wallered" him, but he was still in his sulk, and so I didn't ride him.

We all went to the meeting held by the Missionaries at the schoolhouse. I was deeply impressed by the calm assurance, the childlike faith, the absolute unwavering certainty of all of those people that the doctrine of the Latter-day Saints is so complete and soul-satisfying. And the men didn't rave and rant around to prove their statements by noise—the way I've heard a lot of Gentiles do. They made no statement without substantiating it conclusively from the *Bible itself*. By George, they surely know the Bible as well as the "Book of Mormon" and "The Pearl of Great Price." And they showed results.

Friday, the 17th:

I went out early to get my bronc. I "wallered" him some more and then let him stand under the shed for the day, just to make him mad. He sure was gentle, though. I could do anything with him.

Fred left again for Holbrook and Bill went with him. The Missionaries departed for Snowflake, too. After lunch I settled myself for a "reading," but Barr hollered for me to come over and watch some fun. He was going to ride Old Bill for the first time. Well, the darn horse never took a jump. Then I saddled Spunk and rode him—gave him his first lesson in carrying someone at a trot and lope. He sure is going to be a wonder.

I helped Barr shoe Midnight and started home for my book—"K" by Mary Roberts Rinehart—but it was not to be.

Mrs. Owens called me in to play the piano for several of her friends at her afternoon party. I had a peach of a time, naturally.

I stayed up to the ungodly hour of eleven reading. Such indulgence!

Saturday, the 18th:

I finished "K." It's a blame good book. By the time I finished, Fred arrived with two whole letters and a postal. Gosh, it was thrilling!

We started preparations for a trip immediately. Wilma and the kids, with all of the provisions and beds, left for Gentry Ranger Station in the flivver. Fred, Bill, and I rode three horses and took two pack horses—just to give us the experience with them. We left in a teeming rain—our marvelous luck, for rain is a blessing from heaven here.

We arrived at Baca's ranch at dark and found Wilma waiting for us. They fed us and insisted that we sleep there. So we had another wonderful reception and met some more fine people. Western hospitality is as real as southern hospitality is supposed to be—*nothing* is too much trouble.

Sunday, the 19th:

A wonderful day, clear and cool and divinely green and baby blue and filmy white. It was *so* good to be alive! We started for Gentry Ranger Station and the ride was as nearly perfect as it could be. Great massive pine woods with the road winding up and down little ridges of quaking aspens! Gee, something I've always dreamed about. We just yelled shamelessly for sheer joy.

We climbed Gentry lookout, then on to the O. W. Ranch. The Wallaces fed us and sent us on our way rejoicing. They have a wonderful ranch set on a raised mound in the middle of a natural basin at the junction of about five canyons, and they *always* have water!

Fred and Wilma rode on while Bill and I explored. Of course it rained galore and lightninged and thundered and we got the wrong road. But we sure had fun. We went nearly thirty-five miles, and the horses were tired, but we—well, we're used to it now. We found the folks camped near the station waiting supper for us. Then after some real western bull stories we were ready for a soft, fragrant bed of pine needles under the yellow pines!

Monday, the 20th:

As soon as breakfast was over it began to rain and we all took refuge in the Ranger Station. I braided the bridle reins and the others cut cow's heads for something to do. Then the rangers started to come in, all soaking wet of course. We talked and they played cards all day, and I read a good yarn.

The rain stopped along in the afternoon and Bill and I rode out in the dripping, cool, green world. It all smelled so good and was so refreshing. We went to bed in that wonderful little bed underneath the pines!

Tuesday, the 21st:

Fred and Wilma drove back in the flivver, while Bill and I brought the five horses home. Old Midnight was tied to Major's tail, and the dignity of both suffered accordingly. We reached the ranch a little after one and ate a lot! Then we loafed and read, and I stayed up fairly late that night to finish "Captain Macklin" by Davis.

Wednesday, the 22nd:

Bill and I went out to get our forgotten broncs and spent the rest of the morning working them. Spunk was wild as a billy goat and sure kicked to kill, but after a hard scrap he gave in and was nearly as gentle as before I left. I rode him and tried out his gaits, and he sure has the possibilities.

After lunch I went to Mrs. Owen's and played the piano, and talked with her of literature. She is the school teacher and is mighty nice. Then I wrote letters and ate supper and was ready for my bronc again. He was fine, and I took him out alone. I predict that he will be the kids' pony—he is so gentle and tiny. I slept out under the trees and my slumber was sweet indeed.

To Girl

Last Saturday Fred and Wilma, the kids and Bill and I went on a camping trip—to the most beautiful spot in Arizona. It must be. Wilma drove the flivver with the kids, the food, and the blankets, while we three took the ponies and two pack horses to carry grain for the mounts and to give us experience handling them.

I can't begin to tell you of the trip, the folks we met, the ranches we saw—seventy-five miles from the railroad!—the beauty of the country. A Zane Grey novel? I'll say; only much better because his were all exaggerated stories of blood and thunder and this was calm and quiet, and friendly people. And of course I was the hero. Do you ever imagine—but of course you do. Well, the things you went through this last week-end with me were truly remarkable. I saved your life a hundred times and fought everything from lions to Indians and built a dozen cabins for you, and died no less than five deaths. George, it was fun! But I always had to wake up.

Zane Grey again—we crossed a little wooded ridge, fragrant with cedar and juniper, and went down into the wash on the other side. The cedars had stopped and their place was taken by tall, willowy wild walnuts. The air was filled with a sickening sweet smell like banana oil, and the pungent odor of pitch. We were suddenly in the yellow pines, and the sun on the orange bark, the green of their needles, the flaming sky—was a Maxfield Parrish, if anyone could paint it. And *then*, like a new picture in a kaleidoscope, we were in a cool, dainty grove of quaking aspens, tremulous leaves nearly still—oh, heavenly cool with a little gurgling stream. And the horses put grateful noses in the water and splashed to their hearts' content for a few minutes.

Then the march was taken up, and for another long time the only sounds were hoofs pattering on stones, creaking leather, the snorts of the horses and the first calls of the night birds—glory be, it's true!

But we didn't get back until Fred had been gone with the mail for hours. (He came back first in the car, and Bill and I brought the ponies home.)

My bronc tried to kill me today because he was neglected over the week-end. He has given in after a hard all-morning fight, and I rode him—tired him out. And since lunch I have played the Owen's piano (mostly the serenade from the "Student Prince"), and read Kipling's "L'Envoi"—do you know it?—"When earth's last picture is painted—"

Thursday, the 23rd:

Bill and I went for our broncs right after breakfast. Spunk looked like a Shetland pony beside Old Bill, but good things are apt to come in small packages. He was gentler than ever, and I rode him all around. We got in a bunch of the Flake mares, and branded a colt and then Lavon, Bill, and I drove them down to the Reedhead Tank before lunch. Spunk managed beautifully, and I am hopelessly proud of him.

After lunch I wrote a bunch of letters and worked on my rawhide quirt. I am growing dreadfully lazy, but am sure that I am gaining weight as well as experience.

I didn't ride Spunk again. I just led him around and wallered him a bit, then I turned him loose until next Monday.

A letter to the Chaplain at Lafayette

Dear Chaplain:

How are you after all this time—some six weeks that seem like six months? Gosh, I s'pose I'll have to come back to college some day, too, and in some ways I hate the thought of it. The country is so cool and healthful, and I sleep so much—from about nine to seven!—and eat like a horse, and work and *live*, and have such a glorious time withal that a winter in the city and the sophistication of the people there is nearly more than I want to stand.

But shucks! that will come later. Now I ride and break broncs, and punch cows, and do most everything once at least that a cowboy has to do. You know, when I'm considering the things I'd like to do I must include the "profession" of being a cowman.

I'm living with and in the midst of Mormons. They are

the most marvelous people in the world, bar none, and as long as I haven't seen all the people in the world, I can say that. Just wait until I begin to tell you of them and what they believe. By George, if Gentiles were only taught half as well we'd be better off!

My best to Mrs. Speer and that blessed baby of yours. I am looking forward to seeing you all again sometime in September. Loads of luck to you the rest of the summer.

Dearest Family,

I'm so sorry that I missed the last post, but we were away on a pack horse trip and didn't get back until too late.

Just so I will have something to remind me of the days I've spent here, I've kept a diary. I'm sending the first twelve pages for the first month and I hope you can wade through 'em.

Tomorrow morning early I go to Snowflake with Barr and Grace. You know the 24th is the anniversary of the day Brigham Young founded Salt Lake City in 1847, so they have their big celebration—just like our Fourth of July. And I'm to meet the rest of these people that I have come to love so well. More and more I'm learning to give them my respect and love and they are sure wonderful to me. So I shall send you a card from Snowflake saying that I've turned Mormon probably!

To Girl

Friday I drove down to Snowflake with Barr and Grace and the kids. The town was founded many years ago by Grandfather Flake who is now eighty-seven. Only two or three years ago he stopped riding a horse! He was one of the few polygamists—had two wives and twelve children. Now he has over *300* living *blood* relations and with the "in-laws" some 375! And he talked to us and told us of the day he found the valley and settled that country. Why, it was like a romance—it *was* a romance.

We had a pioneer's breakfast cooked and served on top of the hill above Snowflake to some 300 people. Biscuits, beef, gravy, and bread. It was cooked well. Then we all paraded down to the Stake House (Mormon Districts are called "Stakes"), where there was a pioneer's meeting.

The meeting was opened with a prayer thanking God for giving the pioneers a safe journey across the desert. It was all carried out that way, and some of the old men and women got up and told of personal experiences. I was thrilled.

Then Marsh Flake got me and dragged me up to Taylor, three miles away, for a barbecue. It was sure good meat. We hung around a while and I met some cowboys that I knew, so we had a lot of fun.

Then back to Snowflake for the program—races, contests, etc. It was late when all that was over. I ate at Grace's brother's house and slept at Father Turley's. *Everybody* was so good to me! I was about the only Gentile in the town and they treated me like the best of their own people. Someone was always at my elbow showing me around and introducing me to his friends.

That night my dress clothes came. Fred had them sent up from the Mileses, so I went to the dance. I met Linnie Fillerup, Wilma's sister, and stayed with her most of the time. She's eighteen, pretty, sensible, and at Flagstaff Normal—not bad! So again I had a knockout time.

Saturday morning I read "The Melting Pot" by Zangwill. I've always wanted to read it. In the afternoon I went up to the Fillerup's. Mr. and Mrs. are *delightful*. Gosh, you'd love *her*. You know, she has thirteen children, no one in the family has ever died, they are all strong and good looking and have good educations, and she looks not more than forty-five herself and is healthy and well. Do you wonder that I consider the Mormon women one of the seven wonders of the world? The Mormons have the highest birth rate and the lowest death rate of any people in the world, and most of them are *good* kids!

Linnie and I made ice cream, and then I sought the piano. About four hours later I came to and found most of them listening. I sure had fun.

Then Lawrence Smith came along in his car and took Linnie and me to the dance in Holbrook. Fun? I met the whole Miles family and danced every set and when time came to leave I was sure tired out.

Sunday was Mormon conference and both morning and afternoon I went to church. By now I have a fairly good understanding of their religion—far better than I have of our own, I must admit. But don't worry, I'm not going to change this summer!

So we came home, and I sure had a marvelous time. I have made a beautiful pair of cow's horns for you, and I'll send them home soon. Also I'm making a quirt and a lot of other foolishness. Oh, I may learn something yet!

Sunday, the 26th:

While we were having supper there was a roar that shook

Spunk fighting his first rope

". . . and then I got on my first bronc."

the building—the flood was on us! The old wash sure was filled. I went to sleep with the swirling waters not ten feet away.

Monday, the 27th:

I cleaned up the bungalow and cooked myself some breakfast before Fred and Wilma hove into sight. Then I worked on the cow's horns and finished them. I'll send them to Mother.

After lunch Barr and I chinked my cabin with lath—took us all afternoon. And while Fred and Wilma sat in front of the open fire at night (for it was very cold), I went to bed—I was too lonely!

Tuesday, the 28th:

I started my quirt and then wrote a bunch of letters. After lunch I went out to Spunk—had to rope him, the little demon—but he was a wonder and never bucked a bit.

When Barr could get Old Bill ready we went out for most of the afternoon. I put a bridle on Spunk for the first time and he minded a little *bit*, I can tell you. But he is learning rapidly and I sure am proud of him.

Wilma sat at the supper table with me long after we should have been in bed, talking over all sorts of things.

Wednesday, the 29th:

Up late—almost 7:30! Breakfast sure tasted good. I got a rope and practiced for a few hours to get back in trim again. Roped calves and had no end of fun. Then I read "Ransom's Folly" by R. H. Davis, and by that time Fred was back with the mail. I got four letters!

LARRY

I intended to ride Spunk but Barr was shingling his house and it rained intermittently all afternoon, so I played Mrs. Owens' piano and wrote the following poem:

STORM

When I was a child
I would be wakened in the night sometimes
By the fury of a summer tempest.
I would picture the God of the Storm
Opening the outlets
Of his huge lake in the heavens
To flood the earth.
I could see him riding in his great inky chariot,
Throwing a bolt of lightning—
And then thundering across the bridge again
To throw another somewhere else.
Always he rode across the bridge of the sky.
I could see his horses
Frightened by the glare,
Rearing, plunging, kicking viciously,
And his black face scowling terribly.

I would watch the sizzling spark
Streak from his hand,
And wait with wide-eyed tenseness
And thrilling fascination
For the splitting shock of the chariot
Crashing on the bridge—reverberating—
Then the lightning would give out,
And the horses—trembling, reeking, foamy—
Would rumble the chariot slowly
Back to their stable.

Sunday, the 2nd:

In three weeks I'll have to leave for home! That's all right in many ways, but I hate to think of college so soon. Well, there are still three weeks!

Being horribly lazy I got old King, harnessed him up to my saddle, and went for a nice ride. I tried roping off of him but he was spoiled last year and won't go *near* a calf. I contented myself by driving in the cows—to the accompaniment of a gorgeous moon.

To Girl

This morning Barr, Lavon and I left early to round up the Reed cows. We just got back—five o'clock—without seeing hide or hair of them. But it was great sport and we had lunch at a sheepherder's camp, which in itself is an experience. I probably told you of the last time I ate at one.

We rode the last hour in a teeming rainstorm, preceded by hail, accompanied by lightning and thunder all around us, and followed by wet clothes and a drizzle. But Wilma had a fire waiting for me and some nice hot soup, and after I had borrowed some of Fred's clothes I was sure comfortable. Golly, that is my idea of comfort—dry clothes, hot fire, and steaming soup, served by a good-looking lady, even if she *is* another man's wife!

The darn lightning got very familiar in the afternoon. It struck a tree not far off, and when the horses and *us* had quit jumping at the most terrifying crack, I gasped to Barr: "Thank God it missed!" I always feel out here as if it were aimed especially at me. Unholy egotism, you would tell me, I s'pose.

LARRY

Last Thursday I had my hands full with Spunk. I put the bridle on him and waved the quirt that I had just finished in his face. Well, he had about twenty-seven wall-eyed fits and turned himself inside out. Golly, I sure thought I'd struck a match in a powder factory. We raced all around the hills, dodging cedars and piñons with a fine disregard for my sense of balance, and I was sure clawin' leather a few times to stay with him. But I rode him, and since then he's had a lot more respect for me—and I for him! He is gentle now and is the best (worst?) one-man horse I ever saw. *I* can do *anything* with him—pull his tail or rub his hind legs or make any kind of noise, *anything*—but let someone else get within twenty feet of him and he has a wall-eyed fit. I am not taking many chances—not nearly as many as Dad does when he goes into New York. You *know* that I'm careful.

Last night I was riding him again and finally got him so that I could rope off of him. The bridle doesn't bother him so much now. I went out after the milk cows and drove them back by moonlight. Maybe you don't think that it was a lovely scene. Coming down the lane from the west pasture that old silver lady was right in front of me, making deep purple shadows behind the cedars. The cows were clumping along, the cowbell was tinkling, the saddle was creaking. Old Ted, the pup, was trotting along beside us, and the silos and sheds turned white in front of us. Gee, it was a thing to remember, and I guess I always will.

After supper I dragged my blankets outside where I could have an unobstructed view of the Lady, and dropped asleep almost immediately, worse luck. About three this morning I woke up with a face that was rapidly getting wetter. Mechan-

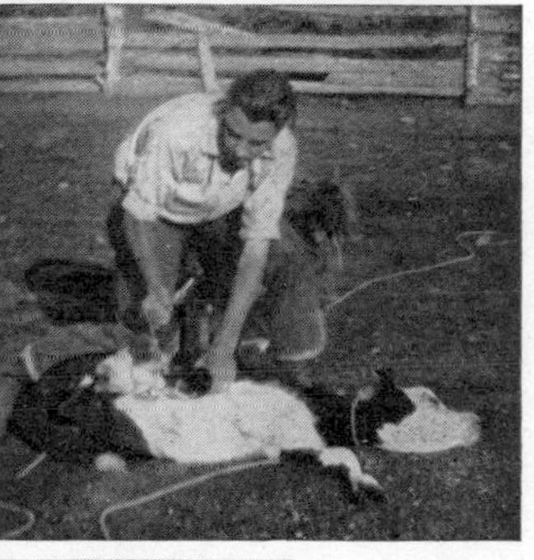

Upper
I tried for a
tying record

Left
Flanking
my calf

Right
Pegging the
required
three legs

Bottom
Darn proud
of my time

ically I rolled the bed up and dragged it back in—and then laughed 'til I was weak at the spectacle I would have presented to an observer, "take up thy bed and walk" effect.

I didn't go to church this morning. I got almost homesick for Dr. Ball and the nice, easy-going religion of Ridgewood for a change. I carved another cow's head and if you don't like the one I sent you we'll change 'em, 'cause this is a dandy.

Listen to this carefully: after you get this letter *don't* write any more to Sundown Ranch, for I will be on the train east, *East!* I leave Holbrook the 19th and get home the 22nd.

Monday, the 3rd:

I intended to take it easy today, but Barr sent over for me. We went down toward Twin Tanks to look for the Reed cows. I rode Spunk to give him some practice, and he behaved himself beautifully. We didn't get back until five and I was nearly starved. After supper it didn't take me long to hit the hay.

Tuesday, the 4th:

Fred's birthday. I sort of fooled around braiding a quirt and fixing up a washstand outside the kitchen door, and other little things. In the afternoon, Wilma went down to Deckers' and after I had read a while I went into the Owens' to play the piano. There was a sudden storm, our little wash flooded, and I spent a busy hour irrigating the orchard.

Wilma came home and made corn bread for me, and it wasn't long before we went to bed. There was a rainbow by moonlight—the first I have ever seen. There was a rain in the west, and the moon was just coming up. We could see evidences of color, too.

Wednesday, the 5th:

I spent more time roping and fooling around. Fred brought some letters and pictures for me. After lunch I got hold of Burrough's "Princess of Mars" and read it, like an *it*. Such rot that I am fascinated once in a while.

Then I hoed weeds with Fred until dinner, rebuilt the dam, and after bulling for an hour, I went to my cabin at the late hour of nine-thirty.

Thursday, the 6th:

Two weeks from this day will find me in Chicago. I rode Spunk and used the bridle a lot; he's gentle as a kitten. The kids will sure have a good pony. Fred and Barr went over to Newman's to get a windmill.

Fred took some pictures of me roping and we came back to a very good supper of corn, corn flakes, and corn bread. We rustled when we got up from the table. We made a fire on the hearth, and Fred read to us.

Friday, the 7th:

I left early in the morning on Spunk with Ted to go to Leo's to return a pair of chaps I borrowed from him. Fred and Wilma went to Holbrook, so I stayed over night at Zeniff. Leo put me to work immediately building a wire corral and some gates. We went down to Carson's water hole and disconnected about 150 feet of pipe to take back to Leo for his dipping vat. We went to bed early after my Texan host beat me at checkers.

Saturday, the 8th:

We were up early and went to work connecting up the pipe from the water hole to the vat. After that all we had to do was fill the latter, using a trench pump. Leo and I took turns all morning and I brought away two little white trade-marks on the palms of my hands!

Shortly after lunch I got Spunk (the blessed bronc came up to me in the corral and Leo nearly fainted) and came the fifteen miles home, driving three of the Reed cows that had broken pasture. I was sure tired and slept the clock around.

Sunday, the 9th:

While the folks were at church I took a shave, shower, and shampoo. Knockout dinner. Before supper I took a good workout chasing around the corn-fields and afterward I finished a quirt I was making. This was the first day I've been in Arizona that the sun hasn't shone at least a part of the time. Rained a bit, too.

To Girl

I laughed at your description of the way you feel when you hear good music. There are times when I could "dance my soul away" too, and I can't think of a better expression of my feelings. But usually I just hurt inside somewhere—same's I do when I see these sunsets. I'm an emotional li'l devil; it takes just a few violins, 'cellos, and such, and I'm blinking pretty rapidly. Fred says that he can't eat a mess of frijoles without wishing that everyone in the world was eating 'em with him. I can't experience loveliness in any form without wishing that you could be with me.

After all, you really only see the decent side of me: I can't expose my *other* side when you're near, in reality or imagination. The mean things always pop out when you're not around. You'd better transform yourself into a pigeon or something and give me the once-over when I'm not expecting you, then you'll get the straight dope about me.

The rattlers that I enclose came from a little two-foot prairie rattler that argued for the right of way down by Zeniff. I went down there to spend two days with Leo, and we had no end of fun and hard work. You'd laugh at the multitudinous things that a cow-puncher has to do. While I was with him, I helped him as carpenter, plumber, mason, rancher, and all-round utility man; cooking, washing, house-cleaning, and I was there a little over twenty-four hours. That is the charm of ranch life—no two days are the same. Compare with that the business life of any one of the men of Ridgewood!

August 11th

Dearest Family,

Just think! a week from today I'll be leaving Airipine. Gosh! it doesn't seem possible that I've been here two months. They have been the shortest two months I've ever spent, and probably the two most filled with the accumulation of new knowledge. The things I have learned and the things I'd like to stay and learn!

But don't think for a moment that I don't want to come home. The only thing that worries me is that I must go back to Easton so soon. Gosh, I hate to think of being cooped up in that filthy city for another eight months, with darn little chance to breathe good air, take good exercise, eat good food, and the rest. But that's all coming, so why look ahead to it?

I have started to write a book of verse! It's to be "Songs of the Arizona Hills" and already I've finished my "Dedication." Of course, there is endless material; all I'll have to do is take my time and keep writing for a year or two—and presto! I'll be an author! Whether financially successful or not is immaterial; it's wonderful practice in word choice for both writing and speaking. I feel as if I've been a sponge, soaking up all the experiences of the lives of these people—and soon I must squeeze the sponge and pass on what I've seen to others.

Physically, I'm as nearly in perfect condition as I ever will be. My shoulders are heavier, my arms are stronger, my chest is deeper. I'm filling out a lot, and some day may be more symmetrical. But it is a health I've never had before; I just get out on the hills and yell for pure joy! I feel like bubbling over and grinning all of the time. Blamed Cheshire cat!

Lord help me, if I had an E. E. right now I think that I'd never come east to live again—awful thought! But there is such a chance for leaders out here, for men who are ingenious, and industrious. Just you wait until I can talk to you of it. At last I have found something that is very near to my heart, that challenges the best sporting blood in me, that fills me with awe because of the possibilities of the undertaking. It is inevitable that the change will hit Arizona; can you realize the thrill when *I* realize that *it is possible* for me to be one of the leaders who *will* make that change? Who knows? Who knows?

Songs of the Arizona Hills

DEDICATION

In praise of vast and endless yellow pines;
Of rocky canyons; tortuous waterways;
Of untold wealth that's waiting in the mines;
Of brilliant nights, and wind-swept, fresh-cleaned days;
Of earth that lives at water's slightest touch;
Of keen crisp harvest time; of quick'ning spring;
Of spreading fields of corn, and squash, and such—
In *praise* of Arizona's hills, I sing.

In honor of undaunted pioneers
Who strove, endured, and died, to make this land;
Of red men, fast decreasing through the years;
Of cowmen who are making their last stand;
Of ranchers who have learned to love a home;
Of lumbermen who make the forests ring;
Of punchers, rangers, herders—all who roam—
Of *folk* in Arizona's hills, I sing.

In expectation of a happier land;
Of irrigation ditch and reservoir
That make prolific soil from barren sand;
And open up earth's richest treasure store;
Of orchards, vineyards, miles of trucking-downs;
Of rapid freighting that the 'plane will bring;
Of better roads and homes; progressive towns—
Of *hope* for Arizona's hills, I sing.

In loving
memory of our
classmates
Larimore
Foster—
Adam Charles
Leader,
this window
is presented
by the class
of 1927

Design by J. & R. Lamb, N. Y.

DEDICATION

Senior Section

Lafayette "Mélange", 1927

WHETHER it is real or assumed, the attitude to life of the college youth of today is characterized by its burden of cynicism. The overworked criticism of the student—that he is a stereotyped product—usually fails to reveal the truth that a large percentage of this sameness lies in the fact that he is unable to rise above an appreciation of the baser human qualities, a selfish, materialistic conception of life, an unintellectual "side-mouth philosophy."

To thinking and unthinking alike, it is rather difficult to understand the Divine Providence that removed one whose outlook and vision so transcended that of the community of which he was a part—one who was an avowed optimist, but not of the ineffective Pollyanna type; and who embodied in all his actions his faith in the innate goodness of his fellows, and his belief that their better qualities would eventually emerge distinct from the background of unformed character. He was not a mere passive model; his participation in many activities was of such a character as to inspire his fellow workers.

Larimore Foster's personality and sincerity in work, play, friendship, made him an object of love and respect. He was an acute thinker, but intensely practical; he was genial, but honest and straightforward in all his relations. His death was a loss that can never be repaired.

LARRY

But the two years he spent with us mean nothing if he is to become only a sentimental memory to us. His life was inspiring, and his death should not end its effect on us. May we ever hold his life before us as an ideal, strive to break away from an outlook purely mundane, and attain to a more spiritual conception of values, a vision of the eternal.

With this hope, the Class of 1927 dedicates the Senior Section of its "Mélange" to the memory of Larimore Foster.

DEDICATION

Frosh Bible—Class of 1930

(A little book of general information given to each Freshman by the Brainerd Society.)

By the death of Larimore Foster, '27, the world lost a true Christian, an inspiring leader, a faithful comrade, and a well rounded man whose character was portrayed in action. Service was the center of his life, yet it was service implicit. We who knew him, though but for a short time, were inspired by his presence. With an unconquerable spirit he fought for the right, and not the least of his attributes was a sense of humor which enabled him to laugh at difficulties. To his memory this book is dedicated.

"We live in deeds, not years; in thoughts, not breaths;
In feelings, not in figures on a dial.
We should count time by heart throbs. He most lives
Who thinks most, feels the noblest, acts the best.

—Bailey "Festus."

"Call it 'The last stand of the cowboy,' "
said Larry as he rode into the sunset,
never to return

TO LARRY

As when the setting sun in the far west,
Touching with golden light all in its path,
Tarries a moment on its way to rest,
Then sinks, in strength, to seek its aftermath;
So went he on an evening, to farewell.
That gleaming life which over us had shone,
Gilding with beauty all on which it fell,
Tarried with us an instant—then was gone.
But even as the sky is glowing still
And filled with gorgeous colors, though the sun
Goes on, his wondrous labors to fulfil:—
So is it with us, now his life is done.
That brilliant, glowing splendor which was his
Lives on in all our lives and memories.

By Mary Hawes

A Student at Ridgewood High School

THE

JOHN DAY

COMPANY

INC.